Women With Adhd

A Woman's Journey to Success

Deborah Kutler

Stay Healthy

Summary

✳ SPECIAL GIFT FOR YOU ✳

Scan me

Scan above to discover these two clues

🔍 **Mystery in the Kitchen**: "Uncover a secret nestled among your pots and pans, where flavors are born and culinary journeys begin. This hidden treasure will transform your kitchen into a realm of simplicity and delight, tailor-made for a masterful orchestrator of meals."

🔍 **Whispers of Culinary Magic**: "Listen for the subtle whispers beside the rhythmic ticking of the kitchen clock, where time and taste intertwine. Here lies a concealed companion, a guide to unlock the magic in your kitchen, a secret ally in your daily dance of life and flavor."

If you Enjoyed it, a review from you will be **greatly appreciated.**

https://www.amazon.com/review/create-review?&ASIN=B0CQ66FSVH/

StayHealthy    

Publisher: misterbondwriter@gmail.com

Foreword

"Women with Adhd – A Woman's Journey to Success " is your personal guide to understanding, embracing, and thriving with ADHD. Tailored specifically for women, this book offers a blend of empowerment, tailored strategies, and real-life insights. Discover how to turn the challenges of ADHD into strengths, navigate life with newfound confidence, and celebrate the vibrant, dynamic woman you are. Your journey towards a more fulfilling life starts here – let's embrace the journey together!"

Introduction

Why This Book Matters

1.The ADHD Landscape for Women

1.a *Brief overview of ADHD as a neurological condition*

Despite its symptoms typically manifesting during childhood, Attention-Deficit/Hyperactivity Disorder (ADHD) is a neurodevelopmental disorder that affects people of all ages. The pattern of inattention, hyperactivity, and impulsivity is persistent and can interfere with daily functioning or development. It's important to note that ADHD is actually a neurological condition that is rooted in the structure and function of the brain, not just behavioral issues.

According to neuroscience studies, individuals with ADHD have differences in brain volume, neural connections, and activity levels in specific regions compared to those without ADHD. People with ADHD frequently experience a decreased activity of the prefrontal cortex, which is responsible for executive functions like decision-making, attention, and impulse control. The disorder commonly causes problems with concentration and impulse control due to this underactivity.

Dopamine and norepinephrine, among other chemical messengers, play a significant role in ADHD. ADHD symptoms can be worsened by an imbalance in the levels of these neurotransmitters, which are essential for attention and focus. Stimulants and other medications aim to raise the levels of these neurotransmitters, which leads to better focus and attention.

It's essential to acknowledge that ADHD is not a universal condition; it manifests differently in everyone. Symptoms may not be as obvious for women as they are for men, which can result in underdiagnosis or misdiagnosis. Inattentive symptoms, such as forgetfulness and difficulty organizing tasks, are more common among women than hyperactive symptoms commonly seen in men.

The myth that ADHD is merely a behavioral issue or caused by laziness or lack of discipline can be dispelled by understanding it as a neurological condition. Recognizing the neurological basis of ADHD is the first step in addressing the condition effectively, reducing the stigma associated with it, and developing targeted treatment plans that consider the unique neurobiology of everyone.

1.b *Statistics on ADHD prevalence in women*

Historically, Attention-Deficit/Hyperactivity Disorder (ADHD) has been perceived as a condition that mainly affects men, particularly during childhood. Recent research and statistics indicate that ADHD is not just prevalent in women, but it is also frequently underdiagnosed or misdiagnosed. About 4% of adult women in the United States have been diagnosed with ADHD, according to the CDC (Center od Disease Control and Prevention. This number is likely overestimated, as many women are not diagnosed because their symptoms are more subtle than those of men.

The gender gap narrows in adulthood, according to studies, even though boys are more likely to be diagnosed with ADHD in childhood. One reason for this is that women often exhibit inattentive symptoms, such as forgetfulness, disorganization, and difficulty in focusing, which are less disruptive and therefore less likely to be identified in childhood. As a result, many women are not diagnosed until they reach adulthood and face challenges that make their symptoms more apparent, such as career demands, parenting, and managing a household.

The underdiagnosis of ADHD in women has significant implications for their mental health. Women with undiagnosed ADHD are more likely to experience anxiety, depression, and low self-esteem. They are also at a higher risk for academic and occupational underachievement, relationship difficulties, and substance abuse.

Moreover, hormonal changes during menstrual cycles, pregnancy, and menopause can exacerbate ADHD symptoms in women, making management more complex. Research shows that estrogen, which affects the release of dopamine in the brain, can influence the severity of ADHD symptoms. Lower levels of estrogen during menstrual cycles or menopause can lead to a decrease in dopamine levels, worsening ADHD symptoms.

Understanding the prevalence and unique challenges of ADHD in women is crucial for healthcare providers, educators, and families. Accurate diagnosis and tailored treatment plans can significantly improve the quality of life for women living with ADHD.

ADHD is often misunderstood, especially when it comes to its manifestation in women. One of the most prevalent misconceptions is that ADHD is a "boy's disorder." While it's true that ADHD is more commonly diagnosed in males during childhood, many women go undiagnosed until adulthood, largely due to the subtler presentation of symptoms. This leads to the erroneous belief that women don't suffer from ADHD, perpetuating a gender bias in diagnosis and treatment.

Another common misconception is that women with ADHD are simply "dramatic" or "emotional." This stereotype can be damaging, as it trivializes the very real struggles that women with ADHD face, such as difficulty in focusing, disorganization, and impulsivity. These symptoms are neurological in nature and not a result of a lack of discipline or emotional instability.

The idea that ADHD symptoms in women are less severe is also misleading. While women may display fewer hyperactive symptoms, the inattentive symptoms they often experience, like forgetfulness and difficulty in multitasking, can be just as debilitating. These symptoms can lead to significant challenges in academic achievement, career progression, and personal relationships.

Additionally, there's a misconception that ADHD medication leads to substance abuse in women. In reality, untreated ADHD is a risk factor for substance abuse, and appropriate medication can actually reduce this risk. Women with untreated ADHD are more likely to self-medicate with alcohol or drugs to cope with their symptoms, leading to a higher likelihood of substance abuse issues.

Lastly, many people believe that ADHD is a result of poor parenting or a lack of discipline. This misconception can be particularly harmful to mothers with ADHD who may already be struggling with parenting challenges exacerbated by their own ADHD symptoms.

Understanding and dispelling these misconceptions is crucial for the accurate diagnosis and effective treatment of ADHD in women. By acknowledging that ADHD affects both genders and manifests differently across individuals, we can pave the way for more inclusive and effective healthcare solutions.

2. The Gap in Existing Literature

2.a *Discussion on the lack of comprehensive resources specifically for women with ADHD*

- Male-Centric Focus: Most existing ADHD studies and resources are based on male experiences, leading to a gap in understanding ADHD in women.
- Late Diagnosis: Women often go undiagnosed until adulthood due to the different manifestation of symptoms, such as inattentiveness and emotional dysregulation.
- Misdiagnosis and Stigma: The lack of tailored resources often leads to misdiagnosis, like anxiety or depression, perpetuating stigmas and misconceptions.
- Inadequate Treatment: Current treatment options, including medication and therapy, are not customized to meet the unique needs of women with ADHD.
- Cascading Impact: The absence of gender-specific resources affects women's mental health, careers, relationships, and overall quality of life.

2.b *Why generic ADHD literature may not fully address the unique challenges faced by women.*

The prevailing ADHD literature, which is largely based on studies involving male subjects, often fails to capture the nuanced experiences of women with the condition. While ADHD symptoms in men are typically overt and easily recognizable, such as hyperactivity and impulsivity, women often exhibit subtler symptoms like inattentiveness, emotional dysregulation, and disorganization. These less conspicuous symptoms can easily be overlooked or misattributed to other conditions like anxiety or depression, leading to delayed or incorrect diagnosis for women.

Moreover, the hormonal fluctuations that women experience throughout their lives, including menstrual cycles, pregnancy, and menopause, can significantly impact ADHD symptoms. Generic ADHD literature rarely delves into these gender-specific factors, leaving women without crucial information that could aid in better symptom management.

Another significant oversight is the societal expectations and roles that women often have to fulfill, such as caregiving and household management.

The executive function deficits that come with ADHD can make these tasks overwhelming, leading to a heightened sense of failure and inadequacy for women. Yet, most ADHD literature focuses on challenges in the workplace or school settings, which may not be the primary areas of struggle for many women.

Additionally, comorbid conditions like eating disorders and body dysmorphic disorder are more prevalent in women with ADHD. However, these are seldom discussed in mainstream ADHD resources, leaving women ill-equipped to recognize and manage these associated conditions.

Lastly, treatment protocols outlined in generic ADHD literature are often one-size-fits-all and do not consider the different metabolic rates or hormonal profiles of women, which can affect medication efficacy and side effects.

In summary, while generic ADHD literature serves as a valuable resource, it often falls short in addressing the unique challenges faced by women. There is a pressing need for more inclusive and comprehensive resources that consider the gender-specific manifestations, challenges, and treatment options for women with ADHD.

3. The Emotional Toll

3.a_Exploration of the emotional and psychological impact of ADHD on women (Pg.70)

The emotional and psychological toll of ADHD on women is a complex interplay of internal struggles and external pressures, often exacerbated by societal norms and expectations. One of the most significant emotional challenges is the constant feeling of being overwhelmed. Whether it's juggling multiple responsibilities at home and work or trying to maintain social relationships, the executive function deficits associated with ADHD can make everyday tasks seem insurmountable.

This sense of being overwhelmed often leads to chronic stress and anxiety, which can further impair focus and attention. Many women with ADHD also experience heightened emotional sensitivity and reactivity, making them more susceptible to mood swings, irritability, and bouts of intense frustration or sadness. This emotional dysregulation can strain relationships, as loved ones may not fully understand the depth or source of these emotional shifts.

Another psychological impact is the pervasive sense of inadequacy and low self-esteem. Despite their efforts, many women with ADHD struggle with disorganization and procrastination, leading to a cycle of self-blame and internalized shame. This is particularly damaging in a society that often equates productivity with self-worth. The fear of judgment or ridicule can also lead to social withdrawal and isolation, further impacting emotional well-being.

Moreover, the stigma associated with ADHD can make women hesitant to seek help, leading to delayed diagnosis and treatment. This delay can result in years of untreated symptoms, contributing to the development of comorbid conditions like depression, anxiety disorders, and even substance abuse as women may self-medicate to cope with their symptoms.

In intimate relationships, the emotional volatility and impulsivity associated with ADHD can create tension and misunderstandings, often putting a strain on partnerships that may already be fraught due to societal gender roles and expectations.

In summary, ADHD has a profound emotional and psychological impact on women, affecting their self-esteem, emotional regulation, relationships, and overall mental health. Addressing these unique challenges requires a multi-faceted approach that goes beyond medication to include emotional support, psychoeducation, and coping strategies tailored specifically for women.

3.b *Real-life anecdotes or testimonials to illustrate the emotional toll (pg.109).*

There is Emily, a 35-year-old marketing executive who has struggled with ADHD since her teenage years, although she was only formally diagnosed in her late twenties. Emily describes her daily life as "walking through a maze with no exit." Despite her high-functioning job, she constantly battles with forgetfulness, missing deadlines, and feeling overwhelmed by tasks that her colleagues seem to handle effortlessly. "It's like I'm always playing catch-up, but never actually catching up," she says. This perpetual state of lagging behind has led to chronic anxiety and bouts of depression.

Then there's Sarah, a 40-year-old mother of two, who says her ADHD symptoms have intensified since she became a parent. "I love my kids, but the constant need to multitask and manage a household on top of my job feels like I'm drowning," she shares. Sarah's emotional sensitivity, a common symptom of ADHD in women, makes her prone to snapping at her children and husband over minor issues. The guilt that follows these emotional outbursts only adds to her stress, creating a vicious cycle of emotional turmoil.

Another story comes from Lisa, a college student who was recently diagnosed with ADHD. She talks about the isolation she feels due to her inability to focus in social situations. "I want to engage in conversations and be present, but my mind keeps wandering. People think I'm disinterested, which is far from the truth." This has led to a decline in her social life, adding to her feelings of loneliness and inadequacy.

These anecdotes underscore the emotional toll that ADHD can take on women in various stages of their lives. The constant struggle to meet societal expectations, whether in the workplace, at home, or in social settings, often leads to a debilitating emotional burden. This emotional weight is compounded by the internalized stigma and misunderstanding surrounding ADHD, making it imperative to address not just the clinical symptoms but also the emotional and psychological scars that many women carry with them.

4. The Domino Effect on Life Aspects

4.a How ADHD affects various aspects of life, including career, relationships, and self-esteem (Pg. 89).

ADHD is not just a condition that affects focus and attention; its impact seeps into multiple facets of life, often disrupting the very core of a woman's well-being. In the career sphere (pg.85), ADHD can manifest as chronic procrastination, missed deadlines, and a struggle with organizational skills. Women with ADHD often report feeling overwhelmed by tasks that their colleagues manage with ease. This leads to a cycle of self-doubt and anxiety, which can hinder career advancement and even lead to job loss in extreme cases.

In relationships, ADHD poses unique challenges. The symptoms often include emotional dysregulation, which can result in mood swings, irritability, and an inability to handle stress effectively. This emotional volatility can strain relationships with partners, children, and friends. Women with ADHD may find themselves in a constant state of tension, unable to fully engage in social interactions due to their wandering minds. This can lead to feelings of isolation and loneliness, further exacerbating emotional distress.

Perhaps one of the most insidious effects of ADHD is its impact on self-esteem. The constant struggle to "keep up" in a neurotypical world can lead to a debilitating sense of inadequacy. Many women with ADHD internalize societal misunderstandings about the condition, viewing themselves as lazy or unintelligent. This negative self-perception is often reinforced by the lack of understanding and support from others, including healthcare providers who may not be well-versed in the unique challenges faced by women with ADHD.

The cumulative effect of these challenges can be overwhelming, leading to a heightened risk of co-occurring conditions like anxiety and depression. Therefore, it's crucial to recognize that ADHD is not just an isolated issue of attention or hyperactivity; it's a complex condition that affects every aspect of life. Addressing these multiple challenges requires a multi-faceted approach that goes beyond medication to include behavioral therapy, emotional support, and lifestyle changes.

This book aims to be a comprehensive guide that tackles the multifaceted challenges faced by women with ADHD. Recognizing that ADHD is not merely a deficit in attention but a complex neurological condition, we delve deep into its various manifestations and their impact on different areas of life.

In the career section, we will explore practical strategies for managing time, prioritizing tasks, and improving organizational skills. We'll also discuss how to navigate workplace dynamics, from dealing with colleagues and supervisors to advocating for oneself in a professional setting. Real-life case studies will provide insights into overcoming career-related challenges and achieving professional success despite having ADHD.

Relationships are another critical area that the book will address. We'll explore how ADHD symptoms can affect emotional regulation and, consequently, interpersonal relationships. Strategies for improving communication, understanding emotional triggers, and maintaining healthy relationships will be covered in depth. We'll also discuss the unique challenges faced by women with ADHD in romantic relationships and offer tips for creating a supportive and understanding partnership.

Self-esteem and self-perception are often severely impacted by ADHD. The book will offer exercises and strategies to rebuild self-esteem, challenge negative self-talk, and develop a more positive self-image. We'll also delve into the importance of self-care and mental well-being, offering actionable tips for managing stress, anxiety, and other co-occurring conditions.

Moreover, the book will feature testimonials and anecdotes from women who have successfully navigated these challenges, offering readers not just theoretical knowledge but also practical wisdom.

Lastly, we will discuss the medical aspects of ADHD, including diagnosis, medication options, and alternative treatments. We'll also touch upon the importance of a multi-disciplinary approach to managing ADHD, which includes psychological counseling, behavioral therapy, and lifestyle changes.

By covering these topics, the book aims to provide a holistic view of managing ADHD as a woman, offering not just coping mechanisms but also a pathway to a more fulfilling life.

5. Empowerment Through Knowledge

5.a *How understanding ADHD can lead to better management and coping strategies.*

Understanding ADHD is the cornerstone of effective management and coping strategies, especially for women who often face unique challenges related to this condition. A nuanced understanding of ADHD as a neurological disorder, rather than a mere lack of focus or discipline, can significantly impact how one approaches treatment and daily life.

Firstly, understanding the neurobiological basis of ADHD can remove the stigma and self-blame often associated with the condition. This shift in perspective is crucial for mental well-being and opens the door for more targeted and effective treatment options. For instance, knowing that ADHD affects executive functions like planning, organization, and emotional regulation can guide you in choosing specific behavioral therapies or medications that target these areas.

Secondly, a deep understanding of ADHD symptoms allows for the development of personalized coping strategies. For example, if impulsivity is a significant issue, techniques like mindfulness and cognitive-behavioral therapy can be more effective. On the other hand, if inattention is the primary concern, strategies may include time-management tools, reminders, or even specific types of medication aimed at improving focus.

Thirdly, understanding ADHD in women specifically can shed light on how symptoms may manifest differently than in men, such as in the form of emotional dysregulation or internalized symptoms like inattentiveness. This knowledge is crucial for accurate diagnosis and treatment, as many women go undiagnosed due to the atypical presentation of their symptoms.

Moreover, understanding the co-occurring conditions often associated with ADHD, such as anxiety or depression, can lead to a multi-faceted treatment approach. This might include a combination of medication, psychotherapy, lifestyle changes, and even nutritional adjustments.

Lastly, knowledge is empowering. The more you understand about ADHD, the better you can advocate for yourself in various settings, be it at work, in relationships, or with healthcare providers. You become an active participant in your treatment, rather than a passive recipient of medical advice.

In summary, a thorough understanding of ADHD is transformative. It not only demystifies the condition but also equips you with the tools and strategies to manage it effectively, leading to a more balanced and fulfilling life.

5.b *The importance of tailored advice and strategies for women.*

- Tailored advice for women with ADHD is crucial due to gender-specific manifestations of the condition.
- Women often experience less recognized symptoms like emotional dysregulation and internalized inattentiveness, making generic advice ineffective.
- Societal roles and expectations, such as caregiving and organization, can exacerbate ADHD challenges for women, necessitating tailored strategies.
- Hormonal fluctuations during menstrual cycles, pregnancy, and menopause can impact ADHD symptoms, requiring gender-specific guidance.
- Women with ADHD face heightened societal stigma, making tailored advice essential for coping with societal judgments.
- Tailored strategies can offer practical advice on daily tasks that are often challenging for women, such as household organization and time management.
- Personalized advice empowers women to manage their ADHD symptoms more effectively, leading to a better quality of life.

6. What Sets This Book Apart

6.a *Unique features of the book, such as evidence-based advice, real-life case studies, and actionable tips.*

This book stands out for several reasons that make it an indispensable resource for women with ADHD. One of the most significant features is its commitment to evidence-based advice. Unlike many self-help books that rely on anecdotal evidence or generalized statements, this book is grounded in scientific research and clinical studies. This ensures that the strategies and recommendations provided are not only effective but also safe and backed by reputable sources.

Another unique feature is the inclusion of real-life case studies. These case studies offer a nuanced look at how ADHD manifests differently in women and how it impacts various aspects of their lives, including career, relationships, and mental health. By presenting these stories, the book allows readers to see themselves in the experiences of others, thereby reducing the stigma and isolation often associated with ADHD. These case studies also serve as practical examples of how evidence-based advice can be applied in real-world situations.

Lastly, the book offers actionable tips that readers can immediately implement in their daily lives. These tips are designed to be straightforward and easy to follow, making it simpler for women with ADHD to start making positive changes. Whether it's advice on how to manage time more effectively, strategies for improving focus and organization, or techniques for emotional regulation, these actionable tips provide immediate value.

By combining evidence-based advice, real-life case studies, and actionable tips, this book offers a comprehensive and tailored approach to managing ADHD for women. It goes beyond the generic advice often found in other resources, providing women with the specific tools they need to improve their lives.

6.b *How the book aims to be a one-stop resource for women with ADHD.*

One of the primary objectives of this book is to serve as a one-stop resource for women with ADHD, eliminating the need to sift through multiple sources for reliable information and guidance. The book is designed to cover all the bases, from understanding the neurological basis of ADHD to providing actionable strategies for daily life management. It aims to be comprehensive yet accessible, making it a go-to guide for women at various stages of their ADHD journey.

The book begins with an in-depth look at ADHD as a neurological condition, debunking common myths and misconceptions specifically related to women. It then delves into the diagnostic process, offering insights into the challenges and nuances of diagnosing ADHD in women, who often present symptoms differently than men. This is followed by a discussion on treatment options, including medication, behavioral therapy, and lifestyle changes, providing a well-rounded view of what comprehensive treatment can entail.

One of the standout features is the section dedicated to coping strategies and life management skills. This part of the book is filled with practical advice, tips, and exercises that women can integrate into their daily routines. Topics range from career and relationship advice to self-care and emotional well-being, all tailored to the unique challenges faced by women with ADHD.

Moreover, the book includes real-life testimonials and case studies, adding a layer of relatability and practical application. These stories serve as both inspiration and cautionary tales, helping readers understand the multifaceted impact of ADHD on different aspects of life.

By offering a wide array of information and resources under one roof, this book aims to simplify the often-overwhelming process of understanding and managing ADHD for women. It aspires to be the definitive guide that women can turn to at any point in their journey, from diagnosis to treatment and beyond.

7. A Note on Inclusivity

7.a *Acknowledgment that ADHD experiences can differ based on other intersecting identities like race, sexual orientation, etc.*

One of the most crucial aspects that this book aims to address is the intersectionality of ADHD experiences among women. It acknowledges that ADHD doesn't exist in a vacuum; rather, it intersects with various other identities like race, sexual orientation, socioeconomic status, and more. These intersecting identities can significantly influence how ADHD manifests and is managed, making a one-size-fits-all approach ineffective and even harmful.

For instance, women of color may face unique challenges when seeking a diagnosis and treatment for ADHD due to systemic biases in healthcare. They may also experience a double stigma—both for having ADHD and for their racial identity—that can exacerbate their symptoms and make coping more difficult. Similarly, LGBTQ+ women may find that societal prejudices compound the challenges they already face due to ADHD, affecting their mental health and access to appropriate care.

The book aims to be inclusive by offering insights into how these intersecting identities can impact ADHD experience. It includes interviews and testimonials from a diverse range of women, providing a more nuanced understanding of ADHD. This is not just an acknowledgment but a deep dive into the complexities that come with having ADHD in a society where multiple forms of bias can affect one's experience and treatment.

By addressing these intersecting identities, the book aims to offer a more comprehensive and inclusive resource. It encourages healthcare providers, family members, and individuals themselves to consider these factors when discussing diagnosis and treatment options. The ultimate goal is to provide a holistic understanding of ADHD among women, recognizing that each woman's experience is shaped not just by her ADHD but also by the various other identities she holds. This acknowledgment is crucial for offering more personalized, effective strategies for managing ADHD.

7.b *Assurance that the book aims to be as inclusive as possible.*

- *Core Tenet*: The book is committed to inclusivity, recognizing that ADHD experiences vary based on multiple factors like race, gender, and sexual orientation.

- Broad Spectrum: Designed to be a resource for a wide range of women, featuring advice, case studies, and strategies that are universally applicable.
- Diverse Voices: Includes interviews and testimonials from women of different ethnic backgrounds, professions, and life stages to offer a comprehensive view.
- Cultural Sensitivity: Addresses how cultural stigmas and systemic biases can affect ADHD diagnosis and treatment, especially in minority communities.
- Toolkit Approach: Offers a variety of coping strategies to suit individual needs, acknowledging that one size does not fit all.
- Aim: Strives to be a one-stop, inclusive resource for all women navigating life with ADHD.
- Impact: By being inclusive, the book aims to make the ADHD management journey easier for every woman who reads it.

8. Your Journey Starts Here

8.a *A motivational wrap-up encouraging the reader to engage actively with the book.*

In a world that often misunderstands and mislabels the complexities of ADHD, this book serves as a sanctuary—a place where you can find not just information, but also validation and empowerment. As you turn these pages, you're not just reading; you're actively participating in your own journey towards better understanding and management of ADHD. This book is designed to be more than a one-time read; it's a lifelong resource that you can return to at different stages of your life. Whether you're newly diagnosed or have been navigating ADHD for years, there's something here for you.

We understand that ADHD is not a one-size-fits-all condition. That's why this book is filled with a diverse range of advice, real-life case studies, and actionable tips. It's a comprehensive toolkit that you can customize according to your unique challenges and strengths. We encourage you to engage actively with the material—highlight text, make notes, and most importantly, apply what you learn in real life. The book is structured to facilitate this active engagement, with summaries, key takeaways, and exercises at the end of each chapter.

We also recognize that ADHD doesn't exist in a vacuum. It intersects with various aspects of identity—be it race, gender, or sexual orientation. This book aims to be as inclusive as possible, acknowledging these intersecting identities and the unique challenges they bring.

So, as you delve into this book, know that you're taking an important step in reclaiming your life from the clutches of ADHD. You're not alone; you're part of a community of strong, resilient women who are rewriting the narrative around this condition. Let this book be your companion and guide as you navigate the often turbulent but ultimately rewarding journey of life with ADHD. Take the leap, engage actively, and let's embark on this transformative journey together.

8.b What the reader can hope to gain by the end of the book.

By the time you reach the final pages of this book, you'll have gained far more than just knowledge about ADHD; you'll have acquired a new lens through which to view yourself and your challenges. One of the primaries aims of this book is to equip you with actionable strategies tailored specifically for women, enabling you to manage your symptoms more effectively and lead a more fulfilling life. You'll learn how to turn what society often labels as 'deficits' into strengths, using your unique neurodiversity to your advantage.

The book also serves as a comprehensive guide to understanding the diagnosis and treatment options available, demystifying the often-confusing medical jargon and providing clear, evidence-based advice. You'll walk away with a better understanding of medication, therapy, and alternative treatments, allowing you to make informed decisions about your healthcare.

Moreover, you'll find solace and validation through real-life case studies and testimonials. These stories will serve as a reminder that you're not alone in your struggles, and that it's possible to lead a successful and fulfilling life with ADHD. The book aims to be a one-stop resource, covering not just medical and psychological aspects, but also practical day-to-day challenges like maintaining relationships, excelling in your career, and building self-esteem.

Importantly, this book acknowledges the intersectionality of ADHD with other aspects of identity, such as race and sexual orientation, providing a more nuanced understanding of your experiences. By the end, you'll have a roadmap tailored to your unique needs and circumstances, empowering you to take control of your life.

In summary, this book is not just a read; it's an experience and a journey towards self-discovery and empowerment. It's a tool you'll keep coming back to, each time gaining new insights and strategies to tackle the ever-evolving challenges and opportunities that come with being a woman with ADHD.

Who This Book is For

This is a comprehensive guide specifically tailored for women with ADHD, with following Target Audiences:

1. <u>The Underserved Demographic</u>
   - Women with ADHD who are often underdiagnosed or misdiagnosed.
   - **Aim**: To fill the gap in resources focusing on women's unique ADHD challenges.

2. <u>For the Newly Diagnosed</u>
   - Women who have recently received an ADHD diagnosis.
   - *Aim*: To serve as a starting point, covering understanding the diagnosis to exploring treatment options.

3. <u>For Those Seeking a Diagnosis</u>
   - Women who suspect they have ADHD but are not yet diagnosed.
   - **Aim**: To guide them through the process of seeking a diagnosis.

4. <u>For Friends and Family</u>
   - People who are close to women with ADHD.
   - **Aim**: To serve as a resource for understanding the condition and offering support.

5. <u>For Educators and Employers</u>
   - Teachers, professors, and employers.
   - **Aim**: To help create more inclusive environments and offer effective management strategies for women with ADHD.

6. <u>Intersectional Focus</u>
   - Readers interested in how ADHD intersects with other identities like race, sexual orientation, etc.
   - **Aim**: To offer an inclusive perspective on ADHD in women.

This book is a one-stop resource for anyone looking to understand ADHD in women, from the women themselves to those who interact with them in various capacities.

How to Use this Book

This book is designed to be a comprehensive yet accessible guide for women with ADHD, as well as for those who interact with them in various capacities. Unlike many other resources that offer a one-size-fits-all approach, this book is tailored to address the unique challenges and experiences that women with ADHD face. Here's how you can make the most out of this book:

1. ***Start with the Introduction***: The introduction provides an overview of what ADHD is, why this book matters, and who it's for. It sets the stage for the rest of the book and helps you identify which sections will be most relevant to you.

2. ***Navigate Based on Your Needs***: Each chapter is designed to stand alone, allowing you to jump to topics that are most pressing for you. Whether you're looking for diagnostic criteria, treatment options, or coping strategies, you can easily find what you need without having to read the book cover to cover.

3. ***Utilize the Actionable Tips***: Throughout the book, you'll find actionable tips and strategies that you can implement immediately. These are not just theoretical suggestions but practical advice that has been backed by research and real-life case studies.

4. *Engage with Real-Life Testimonials (pag.109)*: The book includes testimonials and anecdotes from women who have lived with ADHD. These stories provide a personal touch and offer insights into the emotional and psychological impact of ADHD.

5. ***Keep it Handy***: This handbook is not meant to be read once and then forgotten. Keep it within reach so you can refer back to it as you navigate the complexities of life with ADHD.

7. ***Share with Others***: If you find this book helpful, consider sharing it with friends, family, healthcare providers, and anyone else who could benefit from understanding ADHD in women better.

8. ***Help with the connection***: you will have the ability to connect between the different topics by clicking on the underlined words (in case of Kindle) or by opening the reference page *(example: Engage with Real-Life Testimonials pag.107)*.

By using this book as a guide, you'll be better equipped to manage your symptoms, improve your relationships, and lead a more fulfilling life.

Part I: Understanding ADHD in Women

The ADHD Spectrum: More Than Just Hyperactivity

When most people hear the term ADHD (Attention-Deficit/Hyperactivity Disorder), they often associate it with hyperactivity and impulsivity. While these are indeed core symptoms, it's crucial to understand that ADHD is a spectrum disorder with a range of symptoms and manifestations that go far beyond just being "hyperactive." This book aims to shed light on the multifaceted nature of ADHD, especially as it pertains to women, who often experience the condition differently than men.

Firstly, ADHD is not just a childhood disorder; it often persists into adulthood and can have significant impacts on various aspects of life, including career, relationships, and overall well-being. For women, the symptoms may be less overt and could manifest as inattentiveness, disorganization, or emotional dysregulation, often leading to misdiagnosis or underdiagnosis.

Secondly, ADHD is a neurological condition, meaning it's rooted in brain chemistry and function. It's not a result of laziness, lack of discipline, or poor upbringing, as some misconceptions suggest. Understanding this can help remove the stigma often associated with the disorder and lead to more effective treatment options.

Thirdly, comorbidity is common with ADHD. Many women with ADHD also struggle with other conditions like anxiety, depression, or learning disabilities, which can complicate diagnosis and treatment. Being aware of these overlapping conditions is essential for a holistic approach to managing ADHD.

Lastly, ADHD impacts not just the individual but also their relationships with family, friends, and colleagues. The emotional toll can be significant, leading to feelings of inadequacy, low self-esteem, and even social isolation.

Understanding ADHD as a spectrum disorder is crucial for effective diagnosis and treatment, especially for women who may not exhibit the "classic" symptoms of hyperactivity or impulsivity. This book aims to provide a comprehensive look at ADHD, offering evidence-based advice, real-life case studies, and actionable tips tailored specifically for women.

Section	Description
Nature of ADHD	ADHD is a spectrum disorder with a range of symptoms, not limited to hyperactivity and impulsivity.
Persistence into Adulthood	ADHD often continues into adulthood, affecting career, relationships, and overall well-being.
Gender Differences	Women may experience ADHD differently than men, often leading to misdiagnosis or underdiagnosis.
Neurological Basis	ADHD is a neurological condition, not a result of laziness or lack of discipline.
Comorbidity (pg.33)	ADHD often coexists with other conditions like anxiety, depression, or learning disabilities.
Emotional Impact	The disorder can have a significant emotional toll, affecting self-esteem and social interactions.
Importance of Understanding	Understanding ADHD as a spectrum disorder is crucial for effective diagnosis and treatment.

This table summarizes the key aspects of ADHD as a spectrum disorder, emphasizing its complexity and the need for a nuanced understanding, especially when it comes to diagnosing and treating women.

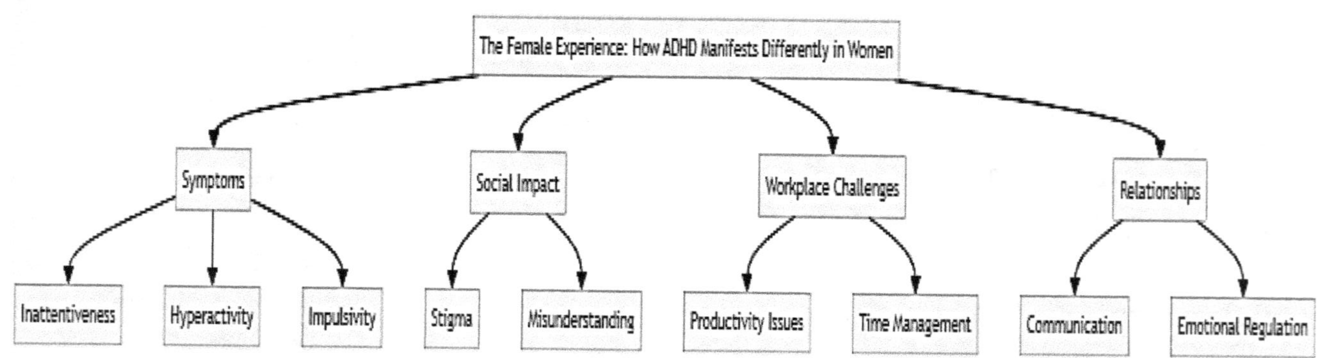

The Female Experience: How ADHD Manifests Differently in Women
Symptoms
Social Impact
Workplace Challenges
Relationships
Inattentiveness
Hyperactivity
Impulsivity
Stigma
Misunderstanding
Productivity Issues
Time Management
Communication
Emotional Regulation

The Female Experience: How ADHD Manifests Differently in Women

The experience of ADHD is not monolithic; it varies from person to person and can manifest differently based on various factors, including gender. For women, ADHD often presents itself in ways that diverge from the stereotypical hyperactive-impulsive behavior commonly associated with the condition. This divergence can lead to underdiagnosis or misdiagnosis, as many healthcare professionals still rely on criteria that have been historically based on male-centric research.

In women, ADHD symptoms often manifest as inattentiveness, disorganization, and emotional dysregulation rather than overt hyperactivity. This can include difficulty in maintaining focus, forgetfulness, and struggle with executive functions like planning and time management. Emotional symptoms may include heightened sensitivity to criticism, intense mood swings, and chronic feelings of being overwhelmed. These symptoms can often be misinterpreted as anxiety or depression, leading to incorrect treatment plans that fail to address the root issue.

Moreover, societal expectations placed on women to be organized caregivers and multitaskers can exacerbate the stress and challenges faced by women with ADHD. This societal lens often leads to internalized feelings of inadequacy and failure, further complicating the emotional landscape of women dealing with the condition.

Understanding these gender-specific manifestations is crucial for accurate diagnosis and effective treatment. It allows for a more nuanced approach that takes into account the unique challenges faced by women with ADHD, including hormonal fluctuations that can affect symptom severity. Tailoring treatment plans to address these specific needs can significantly improve the quality of life for women living with ADHD.

Masking (Behavior)

Masking is a term often used to describe a situation where an individual with ADHD (or another neurodevelopmental condition like autism) consciously or unconsciously conceals or suppresses their symptoms to blend into social situations. This can involve mimicking behaviors, suppressing impulsive reactions, or hiding difficulties with attention and focus.

For women with ADHD, masking can be particularly common due to social pressures and expectations. Women are often expected to be organized, attentive, and socially intuitive, which can be challenging for those with ADHD. As a result, they might develop strategies to hide their symptoms, which can be mentally and emotionally exhausting.

Masking can lead to a person feeling isolated or inauthentic because they are not interacting with the world in a way that reflects their true self. It can also contribute to a delay in diagnosis, as the individual may appear to function well in social settings despite internal struggles.

Long-term masking can have several negative consequences, including increased anxiety, depression, and a loss of identity. It can also lead to burnout because of the constant effort required to maintain the facade. Recognizing and understanding the concept of masking is important for mental health professionals to provide appropriate support and for individuals to develop coping strategies that allow them to be more authentic in their interactions.

Stimming:(Behavior)

Stimming, short for self-stimulatory behavior, is a term often associated with autism, but it can also be relevant to ADHD and other neurodevelopmental disorders. Stimming refers to specific behaviors that are done to stimulate the senses or to soothe or express emotions. These behaviors can be visual, auditory, tactile, olfactory, or involve movement.

For individuals with ADHD, stimming might manifest as:

1. Fidgeting: This is perhaps the most common form of stimming associated with ADHD. It can include tapping feet, playing with hair, or drumming fingers on surfaces.

2. Movement: Pacing, rocking, or shifting from one foot to the other can be ways to manage restlessness or excess energy.

3. Verbal Sounds: Making noises, humming, or talking to oneself can be a form of auditory stimulation.

4. Touch: Rubbing or scratching the skin, twirling hair, or touching certain textures can provide comforting tactile feedback.

Stimming behaviors in ADHD are often a way to self-regulate and can help increase focus and concentration, manage anxiety, or simply provide a way to release excess energy. These behaviors are generally harmless, but they can sometimes be disruptive or socially stigmatized, which is why they are often noticed and commented on by others.

Understanding stimming in the context of ADHD is important for creating supportive environments where individuals can engage in behaviors that help them self-regulate without shame or embarrassment. It's also crucial for helping those with ADHD find appropriate and less disruptive ways to manage their symptoms, especially in settings like the classroom or workplace where certain stimming behaviors might be less acceptable.

ADHD and Hormones: The Menstrual Cycle, Pregnancy, and Menopause

The connection between ADHD and hormonal changes in women is a complex and often underappreciated aspect of the disorder. Hormones such as estrogen and progesterone play a meaningful role in modulating neurotransmitters like dopamine, which is directly linked to attention and focus. During different phases of the menstrual cycle, pregnancy, and menopause, these hormone levels fluctuate, leading to varying ADHD symptoms.

When estrogen and progesterone levels drop during the luteal phase of the menstrual cycle, many women report an increase in their ADHD symptoms. This can manifest as increased impulsivity, emotional volatility, and difficulties with concentration. ADHD symptoms can be exacerbated or mitigated by the hormone surge during pregnancy, making it more difficult for expectant mothers to manage the condition. Postpartum depression and heightened ADHD symptoms can result from the sudden drop in hormone levels, making it necessary to monitor and intervene.

Menopause brings its own set of challenges. During this phase, many women report experiencing 'brain fog', forgetfulness, and increased distractibility due to the decline in estrogen levels. Hormone Replacement Therapy (HRT) has been considered as a treatment option, but its efficacy in managing ADHD symptoms is still under study, and it comes with its own set of risks and side effects.

Understanding the interplay between ADHD and hormones is crucial for women as it allows for more personalized treatment strategies. Providing comprehensive care requires a multi-disciplinary approach that includes gynecologists, endocrinologists, and mental health professionals. More research and awareness is needed in this area, as it holds the key to improving the quality of life for women with ADHD across various life stages.

The Misdiagnosis Trap: Anxiety, Depression, and Other Conditions

Misdiagnosing women with ADHD is a significant concern due to their symptoms often overlap with other conditions, including anxiety and depression. The result of this can be years of incorrect treatment and unnecessary suffering. If a woman has trouble with focus and organization, she may be initially diagnosed with generalized anxiety disorder. Her anxiety can be attributed to her restlessness and difficulty in concentrating, and she may be given medication such as SSRIs or benzodiazepines, but they may not address the true cause of her symptoms, which is ADHD.

ADHD's emotional dysregulation can be mistaken for depression symptoms. Antidepressants may cause women to experience a roller coaster ride, with little or no improvement in their core ADHD symptoms. Delaying the correct diagnosis can also result in medication side effects and a sense of hopelessness.

The diagnostic process becomes even more complicated when ADHD coexists with other conditions. ADHD can coexist with conditions such as learning disabilities, sensory processing issues, or even high-functioning autism, creating a complex clinical picture that is difficult to understand. Women are particularly affected due to their less prominent ADHD symptoms compared to men, making them easier to misdiagnose with other conditions.

The misdiagnosis problem is a reminder that healthcare providers who are trained to recognize ADHD in women should conduct comprehensive evaluations. When treating women for anxiety, depression, or other related conditions, it's crucial to consider ADHD as a differential diagnosis, as highlighted. Effective treatment can include medication, cognitive-behavioral therapy, and lifestyle changes tailored to manage ADHD symptoms, which requires a proper diagnosis as the first step. For women to receive the appropriate care and improve their quality of life, it is crucial to break free from the misdiagnosis trap.

Comorbidity in Adhd

Comorbidity in ADHD refers to the occurrence of additional mental health or learning disorders alongside Attention Deficit Hyperactivity Disorder (ADHD). Understanding these comorbid conditions is crucial as they can complicate the diagnosis and treatment of ADHD. Here's a closer look at three common comorbidities: anxiety, depression, and learning disabilities.

1. Anxiety: Anxiety disorders are highly prevalent in individuals with ADHD. The characteristics of anxiety in the context of ADHD include persistent worries, feelings of tension, and physical symptoms like restlessness or a racing heart. These symptoms can exacerbate ADHD symptoms, making it harder to concentrate or stay organized. Anxiety in ADHD patients often stems from a history of underachievement or struggles with social interactions, leading to a heightened state of worry about future failures or social judgments.

2. Depression: Depression is another common comorbidity with ADHD. It might show itself as a chronic melancholy, a loss of interest in once-enjoyable hobbies, changes in eating or sleep patterns, a sense of worthlessness, or, in extreme situations, thoughts of suicide. The chronic struggle with ADHD symptoms can contribute to the development of depression, as individuals may feel overwhelmed by their difficulties in managing daily tasks or maintaining relationships. Additionally, the impulsivity associated with ADHD can lead to decisions or behaviors that have negative consequences, further contributing to depressive feelings.

3. Learning Disabilities: Learning disabilities, such as dyslexia (difficulty in reading), dyscalculia (difficulty in math), and dysgraphia (difficulty in writing), are often found in conjunction with ADHD. These disabilities can make academic achievement particularly challenging. For instance, a

child with ADHD and dyslexia might struggle not only with the focus required for reading but also with the ability to decode and comprehend text. These learning challenges can lead to frustration, low self-esteem, and avoidance of academic tasks.

In managing ADHD with comorbid conditions, it's important to address each issue individually and holistically. This might involve a combination of medication, therapy, educational support, and lifestyle changes. Recognizing and treating comorbid conditions is essential for improving the overall quality of life for individuals with ADHD.

Adhd and Sleep Apnea

Attention Deficit Hyperactivity Disorder (ADHD) and sleep apnea are two conditions that can impact each other. The illness known as sleep apnea, which is characterized by breathing pauses or short periods during sleep, can cause poor quality sleep, which can worsen symptoms of ADHD. These symptoms include difficulty focusing, hyperactivity, and impulsivity.

In individuals with ADHD, sleep disturbances are common. They may have trouble falling asleep, staying asleep, or may experience restless sleep. This can be due to various factors, including the hyperactivity component of ADHD, comorbid conditions like anxiety, or the effects of medications used to treat ADHD.

On the other hand, sleep apnea can lead to daytime sleepiness, fatigue, and cognitive challenges, which can mimic or worsen ADHD symptoms. This overlap can sometimes make diagnosis and treatment challenging.

Treatment for coexisting ADHD and sleep apnea often involves addressing both conditions. For sleep apnea, treatments may include lifestyle changes, use of a continuous positive airway pressure (CPAP) machine, or surgery in severe cases. For ADHD, a combination of medication, behavioral therapy, and lifestyle modifications, including sleep hygiene practices, can be beneficial.

Some natural suggestions to fix.

> ➤ At least an hour or two before you go to bed, remove any screens from the bedroom and turn them all off.
> ➤ Go to bed at the same time every night. Get up at the same time every morning.
> ➤ Avoid working in your bedroom and, if at all possible, avoid working in bed. Reserve your bed for rest, sleep, and sex.
> ➤ Get regular exercise.
> ➤ Reduce your alcohol and caffeine intake. For those with ADHD, this is particularly difficult because a lot of people attempt to "self-medicate" by using caffeine. However, caffeine has varying effects on metabolism, and it might cause sleep disturbances hours later.
> ➤ In light of your sleep issues, go over your ADHD meds with your physician. Changing medications could be beneficial.
> ➤ Before going to bed, establish a "winding down" ritual that includes soft music, low lighting, and polite chat.

Hyperfocus in Adhd

Hyperfocus in adults with ADHD manifests as an intense, prolonged concentration on activities they find engaging, to the point of losing track of time and neglecting other responsibilities. Symptoms include deep absorption in tasks, often involving digital media or hobbies, and difficulty shifting attention to other, less rewarding tasks.

Hyperfocus can be both positive and negative. Positively, it enables sustained attention for work or creative projects. Negatively, it can lead to missed deadlines and strained relationships due to neglect of other duties.

To manage hyperfocus, adults with ADHD can use external cues like timers or reminders, seek assistance from others to redirect attention, and turn hyperfocus to their advantage by engaging in stimulating and rewarding work. Creating more compelling ways to approach mundane tasks can also help harness hyperfocus productively.

Curiosity
*Blurry Vision

Blurry vision is not typically a symptom associated directly with ADHD. However, there can be indirect connections or situations where someone with ADHD might experience blurry vision.

1. Medication Side Effects: Some medications used to treat ADHD can have side effects that affect vision. Stimulant medications, for example, can sometimes cause changes in vision or dry eyes, which can lead to temporary blurriness.

2. Strain from Hyperfocus: Individuals with ADHD can experience periods of intense concentration known as hyperfocus. If this involves staring at a screen or book for extended periods without breaks, it could lead to eye strain and temporary blurry vision.

3. Co-occurring Conditions: ADHD can co-occur with other conditions that might affect vision. For example, dyslexia is more common in people with ADHD and can sometimes be associated with visual stress that might affect how a person perceives text, potentially leading to blurred vision.

4. Neglect of Health Maintenance: Sometimes, individuals with ADHD may neglect regular health check-ups due to difficulties with scheduling, time management, or forgetfulness. This can lead to uncorrected vision problems that cause blurry vision.

5. Stress and Fatigue: ADHD can contribute to higher levels of stress and fatigue, which can, in turn, affect various bodily functions, including vision.

It's crucial for someone with ADHD to consult with a healthcare professional to determine the cause of blurry vision. Their medication, vision correction, or another health issue could be the cause.

ADHD and Intersectionality: The Experience of Women of Color

The experience of ADHD is not monolithic; it intersects with various aspects of identity, including race and ethnicity. For women of color, navigating ADHD comes with its own unique set of challenges that are often overlooked in mainstream discussions about the condition. The concept of intersectionality helps us understand how several forms of social stratification, such as race, gender, and disability, intersect to create a complex web of discrimination or disadvantage.

Women of color with ADHD face a double bind of racial and gender bias that can make their journey to diagnosis and treatment more complicated. Cultural stereotypes about who "should" have ADHD often exclude women of color, leading to underdiagnosis or misdiagnosis. For example, ADHD is often stereotypically associated with white males, which means that symptoms in women of color may be dismissed or attributed to other factors like laziness or lack of discipline.

Additionally, cultural stigma surrounding mental health in many communities of color can serve as a barrier to seeking help. There may be a lack of awareness or understanding of ADHD within these communities, leading to internalized shame or reluctance to seek diagnosis and treatment. This is compounded by a healthcare system that often fails to provide culturally competent care. Women of color may find themselves navigating a system that is not only dismissive of their ADHD symptoms but also fraught with racial and gender biases.

Economic factors also play a role. The cost of diagnosis and ongoing treatment for ADHD can be prohibitive, and women of color often face economic disparities that make accessing healthcare more challenging. This is exacerbated by the fact that they are also more likely to be underinsured or uninsured.

Moreover, the intersection of ADHD with other forms of social inequality—like racism and sexism—can lead to heightened stress and mental health challenges, making the management of ADHD symptoms even more complex.

In summary, the experience of women of color with ADHD is shaped by a multitude of factors that go beyond the condition itself. Acknowledging and addressing these intersectional challenges is crucial for healthcare providers, educators, and policymakers who aim to provide comprehensive and inclusive ADHD care.

Part II: Diagnosis and Treatment

Recognizing the Signs: Self-Assessment Tools

Self-assessment tools play a critical role in the initial recognition of ADHD symptoms, especially for women who may have been overlooked or misdiagnosed in the past. These tools serve as a starting point for understanding one's own experiences and can be instrumental in deciding to seek professional help. However, it's important to note that while self-assessment tools can be highly informative, they are not a substitute for a formal diagnosis by a qualified healthcare provider.

Self-assessment tools often come in the form of questionnaires or checklists that focus on various aspects of ADHD, such as attention, impulsivity, and hyperactivity. For women, these tools may also include questions that touch on how ADHD manifests differently in females, such as emotional dysregulation, disorganization, and difficulties with time management. These questionnaires are designed to be introspective exercises that encourage individuals to reflect on their behaviors, thought patterns, and daily challenges.

The utility of self-assessment tools extends beyond initial recognition. They can also be used to track symptom progression over time or to evaluate the effectiveness of treatment strategies. This ongoing self-monitoring can provide valuable insights into how symptoms fluctuate and what triggers may exacerbate them, thereby aiding in the development of personalized coping strategies.

However, there are limitations to consider. Self-assessment tools are subject to personal biases and may not capture the full complexity of ADHD symptoms. Additionally, the stigma surrounding ADHD may discourage some women from honestly or fully completing these assessments. There's also the risk of either over-identifying or under-identifying symptoms, leading to unnecessary anxiety or continued lack of treatment, respectively. In summary, self-assessment tools offer a valuable but limited perspective on ADHD symptoms. While they can help you find a professional diagnosis and treatment, they should be combined with other diagnostic methods to gain a comprehensive understanding of your condition. The key is to use these tools as a steppingstone toward gaining a deeper, more nuanced understanding of ADHD and how it impacts your life.

Professional Diagnosis: What to Expect

A professional diagnosis for ADHD is a multi-step process that goes beyond the scope of self-assessment tools. It involves a thorough evaluation by qualified healthcare providers, such as psychiatrists, psychologists, or neurologists, who are experienced in diagnosing ADHD. The process is designed to be comprehensive, taking into account a range of factors including medical history, behavioral observations, and sometimes even neuroimaging tests.

The first step usually involves an in-depth interview where the healthcare provider will ask a series of questions aimed at understanding the individual's symptoms, challenges, and daily functioning. This is often supplemented by standardized questionnaires that rate the severity and frequency of symptoms. For women, special attention may be given to symptoms that are commonly overlooked in females, such as emotional dysregulation and inattentiveness as opposed to hyperactivity.

In addition to self-reports, collateral information from family members, partners, or close friends may also be gathered. This provides a more holistic view of how the symptoms manifest in different settings and relationships. Academic and occupational histories are also reviewed to assess how ADHD has impacted performance in these areas.

Some healthcare providers may recommend further tests, such as neuropsychological assessments or even brain imaging studies like MRIs, although these are not typically required for a diagnosis. These tests can help rule out other conditions that may have similar symptoms, such as anxiety disorders or learning disabilities, ensuring a more accurate diagnosis.

Once all the information is gathered, the healthcare provider will evaluate it against the diagnostic criteria for ADHD as outlined in the Diagnostic and Statistical Manual of Mental Disorders (DSM-5) or the International Classification of Diseases (ICD-10). If the criteria are met, a formal diagnosis is given, and a treatment plan is developed.

It's important to note that a professional diagnosis is not a one-time event but an ongoing process. To ensure treatment strategies are effective and necessary adjustments can be made, regular follow-ups are necessary. This is especially crucial for women, who may experience fluctuations in symptoms due to hormonal changes or life transitions.

In summary, obtaining a professional diagnosis for ADHD is a thorough and multi-faceted process that provides the foundation for effective treatment and management. It offers a level of validation and understanding that self-assessment tools alone cannot provide, making it a crucial step for anyone suspecting they have ADHD.

Medication: Types, Benefits, and Side Effects

Medication is one of the most common and effective treatment options for managing ADHD symptoms, and it often forms a cornerstone of a comprehensive treatment plan. However, it's essential to understand the types of medication available, their benefits, and potential side effects to make informed decisions.

Types of Medication

There are primarily two types of medications used to treat ADHD: stimulants and non-stimulants.

1. **Stimulants**: These are the most commonly prescribed medications for ADHD and include brands like Adderall, Ritalin, and Vyvanse. They work by increasing the levels of certain neurotransmitters in the brain, such as dopamine and norepinephrine, which help improve focus and attention.

2. **Non-Stimulants**: These include medications like Strattera and Intuniv. They are generally considered when stimulants are ineffective or not well-tolerated. Non-stimulants work differently in the brain and may take longer to show effects.

Benefits

1. **Improved Focus and Attention**: Medication can significantly improve the ability to focus, making it easier to complete tasks and follow through on responsibilities.

2. **Reduced Impulsivity**: Medication can help control impulsive behaviors, which can be particularly beneficial in social and occupational settings.

3. **Emotional Regulation**: Some people find that medication helps in stabilizing mood swings and emotional outbursts, common symptoms in women with ADHD.

Side Effects

1. **Insomnia**: Difficulty in falling or staying asleep is a common side effect, especially with stimulant medications.

2. **Appetite Suppression**: Reduced appetite and weight loss can occur, particularly in the initial stages of medication.

3. **Increased Heart Rate**: Both stimulant and non-stimulant medications can cause a slight increase in heart rate.

4. **Mood Changes**: Some people experience irritability or anxiety as a side effect, which may require adjusting the medication type or dosage.

It's crucial to consult with healthcare providers for a personalized medication plan, as the effectiveness and side effects can vary from person to person. Regular monitoring is also essential to adjust dosages and ensure that the medication continues to be effective in managing symptoms, especially for women, whose symptoms may fluctuate due to hormonal changes or life transitions.

In summary, medication can offer significant benefits in managing ADHD symptoms but must be tailored to individual needs and monitored for potential side effects. It is usually most effective when combined with other treatment modalities like behavioral therapy and lifestyle changes.

Alternative Treatments: Diet, Exercise, and Mindfulness

While medication and behavioral therapy are often the first lines of treatment for ADHD, many individuals also explore alternative treatments to manage their symptoms. These alternative approaches can be particularly appealing to those who experience side effects from medication or prefer a more holistic approach to treatment. Here's a breakdown of some popular alternative treatments:

Diet (pg. 125)
1. **Nutritional Supplements**: Omega-3 fatty acids, zinc, and magnesium have been studied for their potential benefits in managing ADHD symptoms. However, the results are mixed, and more research is needed.
2. **Elimination Diets**: Some people report improvements in ADHD symptoms when they eliminate certain foods or food groups, such as artificial colors, preservatives, or allergens like gluten and dairy. However, scientific evidence supporting this is limited.

Exercise
1. Physical Activity (pg. 117): Regular exercise has been shown to improve concentration, memory, and mood — all of which can benefit individuals with ADHD. Aerobic activities like running, swimming, and cycling are often recommended.
2 Yoga (Pag.71) : The practice of yoga, which combines physical postures, breathing exercises, and meditation, has been found to improve attention and reduce hyperactivity and impulsivity in some studies.

Mindfulness
1. Mindfulness Meditation (pg. 69) : This involves paying close attention to the present moment and has been shown to improve attention and reduce stress, which can be beneficial for managing ADHD symptoms.
2. **Mindfulness-Based Cognitive Therapy (MBCT)**: This combines mindfulness techniques with cognitive behavioral therapy and has shown promise in treating ADHD, particularly in adults.

Benefits
1. **Holistic Well-being**: These alternative treatments often focus on overall well-being, which can have a positive impact on ADHD symptoms.

2. **<u>Fewer Side Effects</u>**: Unlike medication, these treatments usually have fewer side effects and can be a good option for those who are sensitive to medication.

Challenges

1. **<u>Time-Consuming</u>**: These treatments often require a significant time commitment, which can be a barrier for many people.

2. **<u>Limited Research:</u>** There is less scientific evidence supporting the effectiveness of these treatments compared to traditional methods.

It's essential to consult with healthcare providers before starting any alternative treatments, especially if you're already on medication for ADHD, as there could be interactions. Many people find that a combination of traditional and alternative treatments works best for them. However, what works for one person may not work for another, making it crucial to tailor the treatment plan to individual needs.

<u>Here's a table summarizing the alternative treatments for ADHD:</u>

Treatment Category	Sub-Category	Description	Benefits	Challenges
Diet	Nutritional Supplements	Omega-3 Fatty Acids, Zinc, and Magnesium for neurotransmitter function	Improved focus, mood	Limited research
	Elimination Diets	Feingold Diet, Gluten-Free, Casein-Free	Potential symptom relief	Time-consuming, restrictive
Exercise	Physical Activity	Aerobic exercises like running, cycling; Strength Training	Increases dopamine, norepinephrine	Requires regular commitment
	Yoga	Asanas and Pranayama for calming the mind and improving focus	Reduced anxiety, improved focus	Requires practice
Mindfulness	Mindfulness Meditation	Focused Attention, Open Monitoring	Improved attention, less impulsivity	Requires practice
	MBCT	Cognitive Restructuring, Behavioral Activation	Positive thought patterns	Time-consuming
General	Benefits and Challenges	Holistic well-being, fewer side effects	Overall health improvement	Time-consuming, limited research
	Consultation	Consult healthcare providers for a comprehensive, personalized treatment plan	Tailored treatment	Requires medical consultation

This table provides a quick overview of the alternative treat, their benefits, and challenges, helping you make an informed decision.

Body Doubling (Coping strategy)

Body doubling is a strategy often used by individuals with ADHD to increase productivity and focus. It involves having another person present in the same room or working alongside them, even if the other person is not actively helping with the task at hand. The presence of another person serves as a passive accountability partner, helping the individual with ADHD stay on task and maintain motivation.

Here's how body doubling can be beneficial for those with ADHD:

1. Accountability: Knowing someone else is present can create a sense of obligation to work on the task, reducing the likelihood of procrastination.

2. Structure: The body double provides a subtle structure and can help establish a routine, which can be very helpful for someone with ADHD who may struggle with self-organization.

3. Social Facilitation: There is a psychological phenomenon known as social facilitation where people tend to perform better on tasks when they are in the presence of others. This can help increase focus and productivity.

4. Reduced Isolation: For some, the isolation of working alone can be demotivating. Having someone else present can alleviate feelings of loneliness and make the task more enjoyable.

5. Distraction Management: A body double can help keep environmental distractions at bay or gently remind the individual with ADHD to return to the task if they become distracted.

Body doubling doesn't require the body double to interact or intervene in the work; their mere presence is what makes the strategy effective. This approach can be particularly useful for tasks that are mundane, repetitive, or require sustained attention. It's a simple yet powerful tool that leverages human psychology to help mitigate some of the executive function challenges associated with ADHD.

Part III: Daily Life and Management

Time Management: Strategies for the Chronically Late

One of the most pervasive challenges faced by women with ADHD is the struggle with time management, often manifesting as chronic lateness. This section of the book aims to address this issue head-on by providing a range of strategies specifically designed to help those who find themselves perpetually running behind schedule. The goal is to empower women to take control of their time, thereby reducing stress and improving overall quality of life.

The section starts by exploring the root causes of chronic lateness in individuals with Adhd. It devolves into the cognitive processes that make time estimation and prioritization difficult, such as distractibility, impulsivity, and the tendency to underestimate how long tasks will take. Understanding the "why" behind the lateness is the first step in developing effective strategies to combat it.

Next, the book introduces practical techniques to improve time management. These include the use of timers and alarms, creating detailed schedules, and setting realistic deadlines. It also discusses the importance of building in buffer time to accommodate for the unexpected distractions and delays that are often part and parcel of life with ADHD.

The section also covers the psychological aspects of chronic lateness, such as the feelings of guilt, embarrassment, and inadequacy that can accompany it. It offers advice on how to handle the emotional toll of being late and provides tips for communicating with friends, family, and colleagues to mitigate the social consequences of tardiness.

Moreover, the book emphasizes the role of accountability and external support in improving time management. It suggests enlisting the help of a 'time buddy,' using apps that track punctuality, and even seeking professional help if lateness becomes a significant impediment to personal or professional success.

By offering a mix of psychological insights, practical tips, and emotional support, this section aims to provide a comprehensive guide for women with ADHD to conquer the challenge of chronic lateness.

The Root Causes

The root causes of chronic lateness in individuals with ADHD can be attributed to a variety of cognitive and behavioral factors. Here are some of the key reasons:

- **Time Blindness**: One of the most significant issues is the concept of "time blindness," which refers to the difficulty in accurately gauging the passage of time. People with ADHD often struggle to estimate how long a task will take, leading to poor planning and scheduling.
- **Distractibility**: The tendency to get easily distracted is another major factor. Even when individuals with ADHD intend to be punctual, they can easily be sidetracked by other tasks or stimuli, causing them to lose track of time.
- **Impulsivity**: Impulsive behavior can lead to last-minute changes in plans or the decision to take on additional tasks, even when time is already limited. This impulsivity can further exacerbate lateness.
- **Procrastination**: Many people with ADHD are prone to procrastination, often waiting until the last minute to start tasks. This can be due to a lack of motivation, fear of failure, or the need for the adrenaline rush that comes with a looming deadline.
- **Executive Function Deficits**: ADHD is characterized by deficits in executive functions, which include skills like organization, planning, and prioritization. These deficits make it challenging to plan and allocate time efficiently.
- **Forgetfulness**: Short-term memory issues can lead to forgetfulness, causing individuals to forget appointments, misplace items needed to leave the house, or lose track of time, all of which contribute to lateness.
- **Emotional Factors**: Anxiety, stress, or emotional dysregulation can also play a role. The emotional toll of running late can create a vicious cycle, where the stress of being late makes it even harder to manage time effectively.
- **Overcommitment**: Sometimes, the desire to please others or the fear of missing out leads to overcommitment. Taking on too many responsibilities can make it physically impossible to be on time for all engagements.

- **<u>Optimism Bias</u>**: Some individuals with ADHD have an overly optimistic view of what they can accomplish in a given time frame, leading them to overcommit and underdeliver, which results in lateness.

Understanding these root causes is crucial for developing effective strategies to manage time better and improve punctuality.

<u>How To Get Out The Door On Time</u>
Here are the tips for getting out the door on time:

> ***Do as Much as You Can in Advance***: Prepare everything you'll need for the next day the night before to reduce morning stress.

> ***Put on Your Time Glasses***: Use timers or apps to help you understand how long tasks actually take so you can plan better.

> ***Build a Routine:*** Establish a set routine to make transitions between tasks smoother and save mental energy.

> ***Use Cues to Stay on Track***: Utilize visual or auditory cues like post-it notes, sticker charts, or phone reminders to help you remember what needs to be done next.

> ***Incentivize Yourself***: Find rewards that are meaningful to you and use them as motivation to stick to your routine.

These tips aim to help you manage your time better and make your mornings more manageable.

The Cognitive Processes

Time estimation and prioritization are complex cognitive processes that involve multiple areas of the brain and draw on various cognitive functions. Here's a detailed look at the cognitive processes involved:

<u>Time Estimation</u>:

1. ***Working Memory***: This ability allows you to hold and manipulate information in your mind for short periods. When estimating time, you need to keep track of the starting and ending points, as well as any interruptions.

2. ***Attention***: Accurate time estimation requires sustained attention. Any lapses in attention can lead to an inaccurate sense of how much time has passed.

3. ***Executive Function***: This cognitive skill helps you plan, focus, and execute tasks. It plays a role in helping you gauge how long a task will take relative to its importance and complexity.

4. ***Temporal Processing***: This involves the brain's ability to process the concept of time itself. The right prefrontal cortex and basal ganglia are particularly important in this.

5. ***Pattern Recognition***: Past experiences with similar tasks inform your ability to estimate time. Your brain recognizes patterns and uses them as a basis for future estimations.

6. ***Decision Making***: The dorsolateral prefrontal cortex is involved in making decisions, including how much time to allocate to a task.

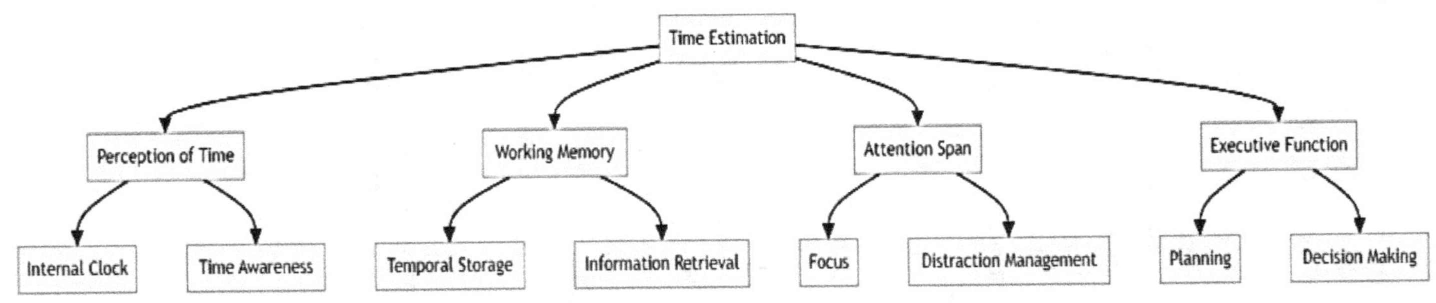

Time Estimation
Perception of Time
Working Memory
Attention Span
Executive Function
Internal Clock
Time Awareness
Temporal Storage
Information Retrieval
Focus
Distraction Management
Planning
Decision Making

<u>**Prioritization**</u>:

1. ***Goal Setting***: The first step in prioritization is setting goals, which involves the frontal lobes. These goals could be short-term ("I need to finish this project by the end of the day") or long-term ("I want to get a promotion within a year").

2. ***Value Assessment***: The brain assesses the value or importance of different tasks. This often involves the ventromedial prefrontal cortex, which plays a role in decision-making and preference-based choices.

3. ***Impulse Control***: The ability to control impulses, often managed by the orbitofrontal cortex, is crucial for prioritization. It helps you resist the urge to engage in less important but more immediately rewarding activities.

4. ***Planning and Organization***: These executive functions, managed by the prefrontal cortex, help you break down tasks into manageable parts and decide the order in which to tackle them.

5. ***Flexibility***: Cognitive flexibility allows you to adapt your priorities as situations change. This involves the anterior cingulate cortex and other areas associated with cognitive control and flexibility.

6. ***Working Memory***: Just like in time estimation, working memory helps you keep track of your priorities and adjust them as needed.

7. ***Emotional Regulation***: The limbic system, particularly the amygdala, helps you manage stress and emotional responses, which can otherwise impair your ability to prioritize effectively.

8. ***Self-Monitoring***: This involves the ongoing assessment of your performance and progress toward your goals, allowing you to adjust your priorities as needed.

Understanding these cognitive processes can offer insights into why individuals, particularly those with ADHD, may struggle with time estimation and prioritization. It can also inform strategies for improvement.

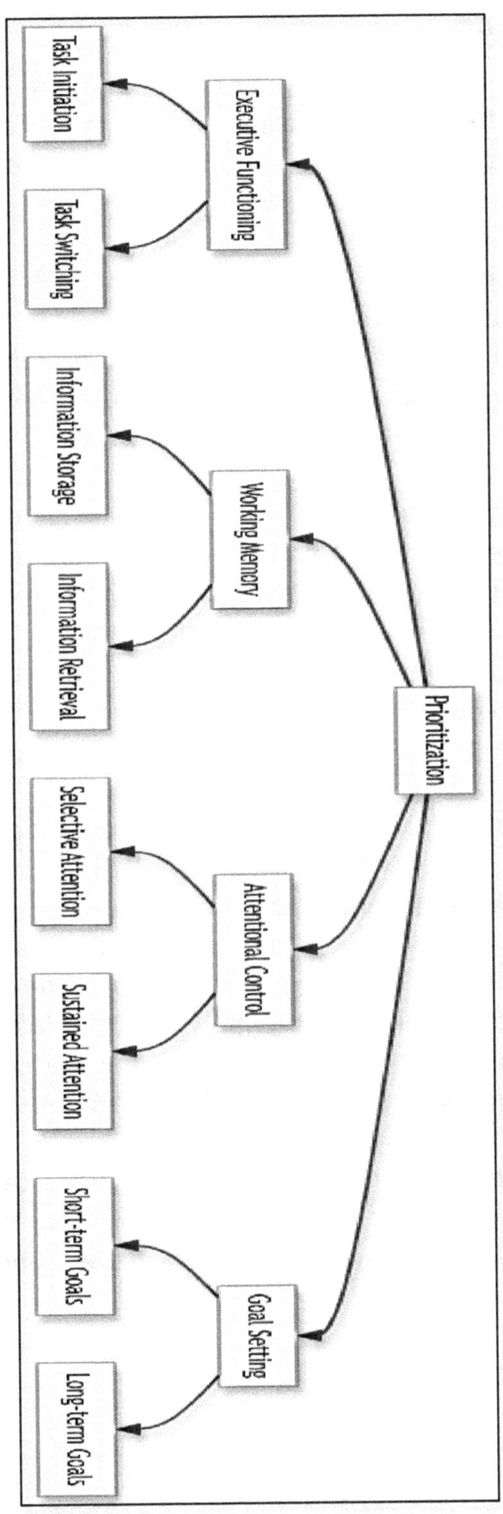

Executive Functioning
Task Initiation
Task Switching
Working Memory
Information Storage
Information Retrieval
Prioritization
Attentional Control
Selective Attention
Sustained Attention
Goal Setting
Short-term Goals
Long-term Goals

Executive Functions

Executive functions are a set of cognitive processes that are essential for the cognitive control of behavior, enabling us to plan, focus attention, remember instructions, and handle multiple tasks successfully. These functions are primarily managed by the frontal lobe of the brain and are crucial for performing activities such as problem-solving, reasoning, and managing time and space.

There are three core executive functions:

1. *Working Memory*: For short periods, we have the ability to hold and manipulate information in our minds. Tools like note-taking apps, digital reminders, and even traditional methods like sticky notes can help improve working memory.

2. *Cognitive Flexibility*: Also known as mental flexibility, this function enables us to switch between thinking about two different concepts or to think about several concepts simultaneously. Mind-mapping tools and brainstorming sessions can enhance cognitive flexibility.

3. *Inhibitory Control*: This involves controlling our impulses and making thoughtful choices. Techniques like mindfulness and meditation can be useful tools for improving inhibitory control.

Several other executive functions derive from these core functions, including problem-solving, reasoning, and planning. Tools for enhancing these functions range from digital apps like time management or project management software to traditional methods like to-do lists and planners.

For instance, the Pomodoro Technique can be used to improve focus and attention span, helping to break work into intervals, traditionally 25 minutes in length, separated by small breaks. The Eisenhower Matrix, on the other hand, helps in urgent-important decision-making, categorizing tasks based on their exigence and importance.

Understanding and improving these executive functions can significantly impact one's ability to function effectively in daily life, particularly for individuals with conditions like ADHD, where these functions can be impaired.

Organizational Skills: From Chaos to Clarity

Organizational skills are a critical aspect of managing daily life, especially for individuals with ADHD who often struggle with disorganization due to executive function challenges. The section "Organizational Skills: From Chaos to Clarity" aims to provide readers with practical strategies to transform their disorganized lives into well-structured routines.

The chapter begins by acknowledging the common struggles that people with ADHD face, such as misplaced items, forgotten appointments, and overwhelming clutter—both physical and mental. It emphasizes that disorganization is not a character flaw but a challenge that can be overcome with the right tools and techniques.

The chapter then delves into various organizational methods tailored to the unique needs of women with ADHD. It covers topics like:

1. *Home Organization*: Tips for decluttering and maintaining an organized living space, including the KonMari method and the "one in, one out" rule.

2. *Workplace Organization*: Strategies for managing paperwork, digital files, and deadlines. It introduces tools like project management software and techniques like batching similar tasks together.

3. *Time Management*: The chapter explores various time management techniques such as the Eisenhower Matrix for prioritizing tasks and the Pomodoro Technique for maintaining focus.

4. *Mental Organization:* Techniques for organizing thoughts and reducing mental clutter are discussed. Mindfulness and meditation are introduced as tools for achieving mental clarity.

5. *Family and Relationships*: The chapter also touches on organizing family life, including managing chores, school routines, and family activities using shared calendars and apps.

6. *Financial Organization*: Budgeting and financial planning tools are discussed to help manage the often-overlooked aspect of financial disorganization.

By the end of this chapter, the reader should have a comprehensive toolkit of strategies and methods to bring order to the chaos that ADHD often brings. The aim is to empower women with ADHD to live more organized, fulfilling lives, thereby reducing stress and increasing productivity.

1. Procrastination
- Struggle: Difficulty in starting tasks, leading to last-minute rushes and stress.
- Tools & Techniques:
  - Time Blocking: Allocate specific time slots for tasks.
  - Pomodoro Technique: Work in short increments with pauses in between.
Pomodoro tecnique - Pag. 58 -

2. Forgetfulness
- Struggle: Forgetting appointments, tasks, or important dates.
- Tools & Techniques:
  - Digital Calendars: Use reminders and notifications.
  - Physical Planners: Write down important dates and to-dos.
The Journal - Pag. 63-

3. Impulsivity
- Struggle: Making hasty decisions without considering the consequences.
- Tools & Techniques:
  - Pause Technique: Take a moment to think before acting.
  - Pros and Cons List: Quickly jot down the advantages and disadvantages.

4. Time Management
- Struggle: Missing deadlines can be caused by underestimating how long tasks will take.
- Tools & Techniques:
  - Eisenhower Matrix: Prioritize tasks based on urgency and importance.
  - Time Tracking Apps: Monitor how long tasks actually take.
Eisenhower Matrix – pag.61 –

5. Disorganization
- Struggle: Cluttered spaces, both physical and digital, leading to lost items and wasted time.
- Tools & Techniques:
  - Decluttering: Regularly sort and discard unnecessary items.
  - Digital Organization Tools: Use apps for note-taking, file storage, etc.

6. Lack of Focus
- Struggle: Easily distracted, leading to uncompleted tasks.
- Tools & Techniques:
  - Noise-Canceling Headphones: To block out distractions.
  - Focus Apps: Apps that block distracting websites during work hours.

7. Emotional Dysregulation
- Struggle: Difficulty in managing emotions, leading to mood swings and conflicts.
- Tools & Techniques:
  - Mindfulness: Practice mindfulness to become aware of emotional triggers.
  - Emotional Journaling: Keep a journal to track mood patterns.
Emotional Journaling Pag. 92

8. Task Switching
- Struggle: Difficulty in transitioning from one task to another.
- Tools & Techniques:
  - Batching: Group similar tasks together to minimize switching.
  - Transitional Rituals: Develop small rituals to signify the end of one task and the beginning of another.

9. Overwhelm
- Struggle: Feeling overwhelmed by the number of tasks or choices.
- Tools & Techniques:
  - Task Decomposition: Break down tasks into smaller, manageable parts.
  - One Thing at a Time: Concentrate on finishing one task before proceeding to the next one

10. Social Challenges
- Struggle: Difficulty in maintaining relationships due to impulsivity, forgetfulness, or emotional dysregulation.
- Tools & Techniques:
  - Active Listening: Practice being present in conversations.
  - Scheduled Check-ins: Regularly schedule time to catch up with friends and family.

By understanding these common struggles and applying the appropriate tools and techniques, individuals with ADHD can significantly get better their daily functioning and overall well-being.

Pomodoro Technique

The Pomodoro Technique is a time management method developed by Francesco Cirillo in the late 1980s. The technique encourages people to work with the time they have—rather than against it. Using this method, you break your workday into 25-minute chunks separated by five-minute breaks. These intervals are referred to as "pomodoros," named after the tomato-shaped kitchen timer that Cirillo used as a university student.

How It Works:
1. **Choose a Task**: Decide on the task you would like to get done.
2. **Set the Timer**: Set the Pomodoro timer for 25 minutes.
3. **Work on the Task**: Work on the task until the timer goes off.
4. **Take a Short Break**: After the timer rings, put a checkmark on a piece of paper, and take a short break (5 minutes).
5. **Take a Longer Break**: Every four pomodoros, take a longer break (15–30 minutes).
Benefits:

- **Improves Focus and Attention**: By working in short sprints, you can keep your mind fresh and focused.

- **<u>Increases Productivity</u>**: It can help you get more done in less time if used correctly.
- **<u>Flexible</u>**: The technique is simple and can be adapted to suit your own productivity rhythms.
- **<u>Reduces Burnout</u>**: Regular breaks can improve mental agility.
- **<u>Track Time</u>**: It can give you a clear picture of how you spend your time.

Challenges:
- **<u>Interruptions</u>**: It can be challenging to maintain the technique in an environment prone to interruptions.
- **<u>Over-Simplification</u>**: Some tasks may not neatly fit into 25-minute chunks.

Who Can Benefit:
- *Students*: For studying and writing assignments.
- *Professionals*: For completing work tasks efficiently.
- *Creatives*: For dedicating focused time to artistic pursuits.
- *Anyone with ADHD*: The structured time intervals can help in maintaining focus and attention.

The Pomodoro Technique is particularly useful for people with ADHD as it turns time management into a structured game, making it easier to maintain focus and complete tasks. It's a simple yet effective way to manage time and improve productivity.

<u>Tab. 1 Exemple Mind Map Pomodoro Tecnique</u>

Step 1		Pick a Task
Step 2		Set a 25-Minutes Timer
Step 3		Work On Your Task Until The Time Is Up
Step 4		Take a 5 Minutes Break
Step 5		Every 4 Pomodoros, take a longer 15-30 minute break

Tab. 2 Example Table Pomodoro Tecnique

Below is an example of a Pomodoro Technique table that outlines steps, times, employment (tasks), and commitments. This table can serve as a guide for how to structure your day using the Pomodoro Technique.

Step	Time	Employment (Tasks)	Commitments
1	9:00-9:25	Check Emails	Respond to urgent emails
Break	9:25-9:30		Stretch, grab a coffee
2	9:30-9:55	Work on Project A	Complete initial research
Break	9:55-10:00		Quick walk, hydration
3	10:00-10:25	Continue on Project A	Draft outline
Break	10:25-10:30		Check social media
4	10:30-10:55	Finalize Project A	Finish and review outline
Long Break	10:55-11:10		Relax, maybe read a bit
5	11:10-11:35	Start Project B	Brainstorm ideas
Break	11:35-11:40		Stretch, quick snack
6	11:40-12:05	Work on Presentation	Create slides
Break	12:05-12:10		Quick walk, hydration
7	12:10-12:35	Continue on Presentation	Add content to slides
Break	12:35-12:40		Check messages
8	12:40-1:05	Finalize Presentation	Review and polish slides
Long Break	1:05-1:20		Lunch break

This table is just an example and can be adapted to fit your specific needs and tasks. The idea is to use the 25-minute work intervals to focus solely on one task at a time, followed by a 5-minute break to relax and recharge. After completing four Pomodoros, take a longer break to rest and rejuvenate.

Eisenhower Matrix

The Eisenhower Matrix, also known as the Urgent-Important Matrix, is a time management tool that helps you prioritize tasks based on their urgency and importance. The matrix is divided into four quadrants:

- Urgent and Important (**Do First**)
- Important but Not Urgent (**Schedule**)
- Urgent but Not Important **(Delegate)**
- Neither Urgent nor Important (**Eliminate**)

Here's how the matrix looks:

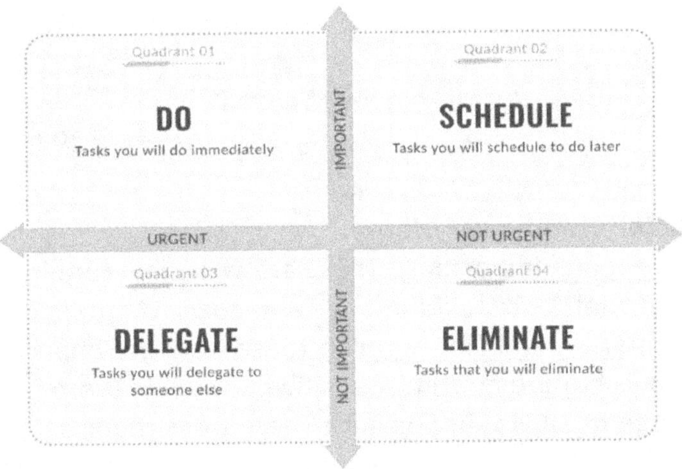

Schedule Example:

Time	Task	Quadrant	Notes
9:00-9:30	Finish project proposal	**Do First**	Deadline today
9:30-10:00	Plan next week's schedule	Schedule	Important for time management
10:00-10:30	Respond to client emails	Delegate	Can be handled by assistant
10:30-11:00	Browse social media	Eliminate	Not urgent or important
11:00-11:30	Team meeting	**Do First**	Discuss project milestones
11:30-12:00	Research for future projects	Schedule	Important but not time-sensitive
12:00-12:30	Lunch	-	-
12:30-1:00	Handle customer complaints	Delegate	Can be handled by customer service
1:00-1:30	Review monthly budget	Schedule	Important for financial planning
1:30-2:00	Casual chat with colleagues	Eliminate	Not contributing to goals

How to Use the Eisenhower Matrix:

Do First (<u>Urgent and Important</u>): These are tasks that require immediate attention and contribute to your long-term goals. Do them first.

Schedule (<u>Important but Not Urgent</u>): These tasks are important for your long-term goals but are not time-sensitive. Schedule them for later.

Delegate (<u>Urgent but Not Important</u>): These tasks require immediate attention but don't contribute to your long-term goals. Delegate them if possible.

Eliminate (<u>Neither Urgent nor Important</u>): These tasks don't contribute to your long-term goals and are not time-sensitive. Consider eliminating them from your to-do list.

By using the Eisenhower Matrix, you can better manage your time and focus on what truly matters.

A Friend On Hand: The Journal

Journaling can be a powerful tool for individuals with ADHD, offering a variety of benefits. Here are some of the advantages and tips for effective journaling:

Benefits:

1. **Improved Focus**: Journaling can serve as a mindfulness practice, helping to enhance focus by anchoring attention on the present moment.

2. **Reduced Anxiety**: Writing down anxious thoughts can help in externalizing and thus reducing anxiety.

3. **Enhanced Creativity**: Journaling can foster creativity by allowing a free flow of ideas, and capturing fleeting thoughts before they are forgotten.

4. **Reduced Stress and Improved Emotional Regulation**: These benefits come by providing a space to process and work through emotions.

5. **Support for Organization**: Journaling can help in organizing thoughts and daily responsibilities, thus contributing to better management of ADHD symptoms.

Tips for Effective Journaling:

1. **Choosing a Notebook**: Select a simple, accessible notebook to eliminate any initial barriers to starting.

2. **Being Authentic**: Write whatever comes to mind without aiming for perfection or worrying about an audience. This will make the process less overwhelming and more enjoyable.

3. **Consistency**: Establishing a routine can aid in making journaling a habit. However, flexibility is key. Finding a routine that works for you, whether it's journaling over morning coffee or in the evening, can be helpful.

4. **Avoid Overthinking**: Write without a censor to allow a free flow of thoughts and emotions. This can help in better self-reflection and self-understanding.

5. **Comfort**: Make yourself comfortable while journaling to promote openness and mindfulness in your writing.

Various methods and types of journals can be explored to find what suits individual needs the best, such as using prompts, maintaining a gratitude journal, or even digital journaling. The overarching advice is to keep the process simple, authentic, and enjoyable to reap the maximum benefits of journaling for managing ADHD symptoms.

Example of Jouranal

How someone with ADHD might structure a journal entry along with explanations of each section:

Date: October 21, 2023

Morning Reflections (8:00 AM)
Mood: Feeling a bit scattered but hopeful.
Sleep: Slept for 7 hours, had some trouble falling asleep.
Today's Goals: Finish the report for work, exercise for 30 minutes, and cook dinner.

Midday Check-in (12:00 PM)

Focus Levels: Struggled in the morning, but it got better after a short walk outdoors.
Progress Towards Goals: Completed half of the report, still need to exercise and plan dinner.
Unexpected Challenges: Got distracted by emails and phone calls, which delayed the report work.

Evening Reflections (8:00 PM)

Achievements: Finished the report, exercised for 20 minutes, cooked a healthy dinner.
What Worked Well: Taking breaks and walking helped in regaining focus.
What Didn't Work: Procrastination in the morning, got caught up in less important tasks.

🏆 🛏 Thoughts and Feelings: Felt accomplished for meeting most of the goals, though a bit frustrated with procrastination. Enjoyed the dinner and felt relaxed afterward.

Notes for Tomorrow:
- Try starting with the most important task of the day.
- Explore a new relaxation technique to improve sleep quality.
- Keep practicing mindfulness to enhance focus.

Gratitude:
- Grateful for the peaceful evening and the tasty dinner cooked.
- Thankful for the support from my colleague in finishing the report.

Breakdown of Sections:
- Date: Keeping track of the date can help in observing patterns over time.
- Morning Reflections: A space to set intentions and goals for the day.
- Midday Check-in: A chance to assess progress and adjust plans if necessary.
- Evening Reflections: Reflecting on the day's achievements and challenges helps in understanding what works and what doesn't.
- Notes for Tomorrow: Planning ahead can assist in setting up for a successful day.
- Gratitude: Expressing gratitude can boost mood and provide a positive end to the journaling experience.

This structured format can be beneficial for individuals with ADHD to organize their thoughts, set and track goals, and reflect on their experiences. However, the format can be adapted to meet individual preferences and needs. The key is to keep the process enjoyable and beneficial, without it becoming a source of stress.

- ***Home Organization: KonMari Method***

The KonMari Method, developed by Marie Kondo, is a decluttering and organizing method that asks you to keep only those items that "spark joy." This method is particularly useful for women with ADHD who may struggle with decision-making and emotional attachment to objects.

Tools & Techniques:

- Categorization: Sort items by category, not by location.
- Joy-Check: Hold each item and ask if it sparks joy.
- Mindful Folding: Fold items in a way that allows you to see everything in a drawer at once.

- ***Workplace Organization***

The workplace can be a challenging environment for women with ADHD due to distractions, multitasking, and deadlines.

Tools & Techniques:

- Task Batching: Group similar tasks together to tackle in one go.
- Visual Aids: Use sticky notes or whiteboards to jot down tasks and deadlines.
- Digital Tools: Utilize project management software like Asana or Trello.

- **Time Management**

Managing time effectively is often a significant challenge for women with ADHD.

Tools & Techniques:

- Pomodoro Technique: Work in short bursts of focused time, followed by a break.
- Time Blocking: Allocate specific blocks of time for different activities or tasks.
- Reminders: Use smartphone apps to set reminders for appointments and deadlines.

- **Mental Organization**

Mental clutter can be as debilitating as physical clutter, especially for women with ADHD.

Tools & Techniques:

- <u>Mind Mapping</u>: Use mind maps to organize thoughts and ideas visually.
- <u>Meditation</u>: Practice mindfulness meditation to enhance focus and clarity.
- <u>Journaling</u>: Write down thoughts, ideas, and feelings to declutter the mind.

- **Family and Relationships**

Managing family life and relationships requires a different set of organizational skills.

Tools & Techniques:
- <u>Family Calendar</u>: Use a shared digital calendar for all family events and commitments.
- <u>Chore Charts</u>: Create a chore chart to distribute household tasks fairly.
- <u>Scheduled Quality Time:</u> Plan regular family activities and date nights.

- **Financial Organization**

Financial disorganization can lead to stress and anxiety, more so for women with ADHD.

Tools & Techniques:
- <u>Budgeting Apps</u>: Use apps like Mint or YNAB for budget tracking.
- <u>Automated Payments</u>: Set up automated payments for recurring bills.
- <u>Financial Goals</u>: Set short-term and long-term financial goals and track them regularly.

By tailoring these organizational methods to the unique challenges faced by women with ADHD, it becomes easier to manage various aspects of life more effectively. These tools and techniques offer practical solutions that can be adapted to individual needs, making daily life less overwhelming and more manageable.

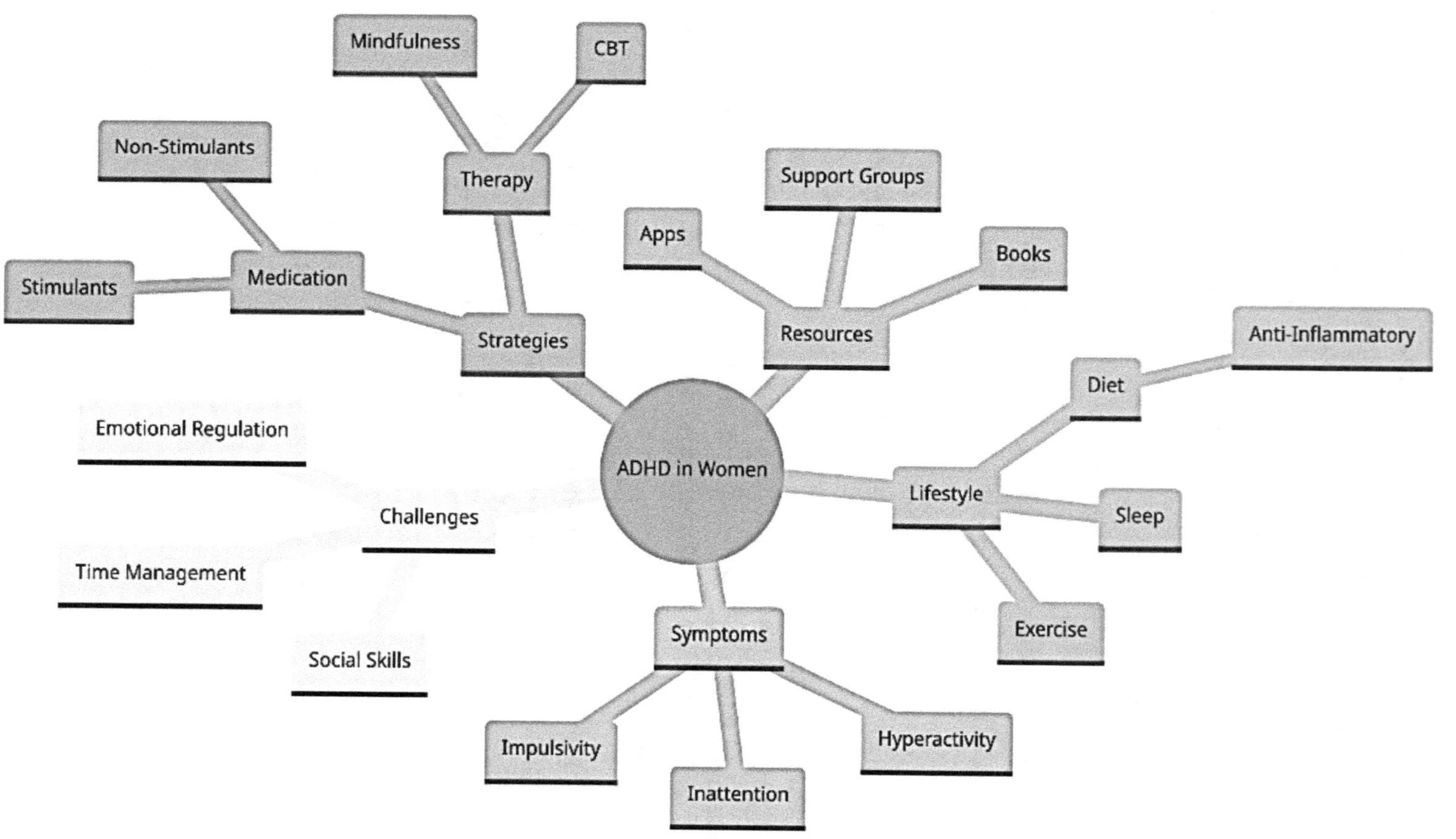

Mindfulness
CBT
Therapy
Non-Stimulants
Stimulants
Medication
Apps
Support Groups
Books
Resources
Anti-Inflammatory
Diet
Strategies
ADHD in Women
Lifestyle
Sleep
Emotional Regulation
Challenges
Time Management
Exercise
Social Skills
Symptoms
Impulsivity
Inattention
Hyperactivity

Mudra Meditation

Mudra meditation involves using specific hand gestures or "mudras" to channel energy flow in the body. The belief is that these mudras stimulate the different parts of the body that participate in breathing and affect the flow of energy in the body, resulting in increased focus and meditation.
Most Common Mudras Meditation for Focus.

1. Gyan Mudra
- <u>How to Do It</u>: Touch the tip of the thumb to the tip of the index finger, keeping the other three fingers straight.
- <u>Benefits</u>: Enhances concentration and memory.

2. Prana Mudra
- <u>How to Do It</u>: Touch the tip of the thumb to the tips of the ring and little fingers, keeping the other two fingers straight.
- <u>Benefits:</u> Increases vitality and reduces fatigue.

3. Dhyana Mudra

   - <u>How to Do It</u>: Put your hands in your lap, left hand under the right, palms facing up, and the tips of the thumbs touching.

   - <u>Benefits</u>: Helps in deep contemplation and meditation.

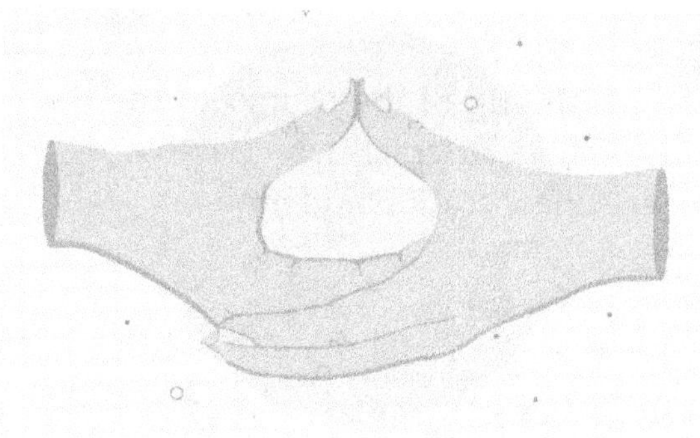

4. Anjali Mudra

   - <u>How to Do It</u>: Press the palms together in a prayer position, usually at the heart.

   - <u>Benefits</u>: Promotes respect for oneself and others and aids in focus.

5. **Buddhi Mudra**
 - <u>How to Do It</u>: Contact the tip of the thumb to the tip of the little finger.
 - <u>Benefits</u>: Enhances communication and improves intuitive communication.

How to Use Mudras in Meditation
1. <u>Choose a Comfortable Position</u>: Sit in a comfortable position with your spine straight.
2. <u>Select a Mudra</u>: Choose a mudra that lines up with your meditation goal.
3. <u>Hold the Mudra</u>: Place your hands in the chosen mudra.
4. <u>Focus</u>: Close your eyes and focus on your breath or a chosen point of concentration.
5. <u>Time</u>: Hold the mudra for as long as you are comfortable, aiming for at least a few minutes.

Yoga Asanas For People With ADHD

Various reasons make yoga particularly beneficial for individuals with ADHD.

1. *Enhances Focus and Concentration*: Yoga often involves mindfulness practices and concentration on breath and body movements. These aspects can help individuals with ADHD improve their attention span and focus, which are typically challenging areas for them.

2. *Reduces Hyperactivity and Impulsivity*: The physical practice of yoga can help in managing the high energy levels and impulsivity often associated with

ADHD. Engaging in yoga poses (asanas) requires controlled, deliberate movements, which can help in calming the body and mind.

3. _Improves Self-Regulation_: Yoga teaches self-awareness and self-regulation skills. People with ADHD can benefit from learning how to regulate their emotions and responses, which yoga facilitates through breathing exercises (pranayama) and meditation.

4. _Stress and Anxiety Reduction_: Stress and anxiety levels are often elevated in individuals with ADHD. Reducing stress and anxiety levels can be achieved through yoga's emphasis on relaxation and mindful breathing, leading to a sense of calm and well-being.

5. _Enhances Executive Functioning_: Executive functions include skills like planning, organization, and time management, which can be challenging for those with ADHD. Regular yoga practice has been shown to strengthen the prefrontal cortex – the brain area associated with these skills.

6. _Improves Sleep Patterns_: Many individuals with ADHD struggle with sleep disturbances. Yoga has the potential to promote relaxation and establish a more regular and restful sleep pattern.

7. _Boosts Physical Health_: Beyond mental health benefits, yoga is also a form of physical exercise that can improve overall physical health, flexibility, balance, and strength.

8. _Provides a Structured Routine_: Individuals with ADHD who often thrive in structured environments may find the structured nature of a yoga practice to be beneficial due to its sense of routine and stability

9. _Enhances Self-Esteem and Body Awareness_: Regular yoga practice can lead to improvements in body awareness and self-esteem. For individuals with ADHD, who may often face challenges and setbacks, these benefits can be particularly empowering.

10. _Complementary to Traditional Treatments_: While not a substitute for traditional ADHD treatments like medication and behavioral therapy, yoga can be an effective complementary approach, offering holistic benefits that address both the mind and body.

Several yoga asanas (poses) are particularly beneficial for individuals with ADHD, helping to improve focus, reduce hyperactivity, and promote calmness. Some of the most notable ones include:

1. *Tree Pose (Vrikshasana)*: This balancing pose enhances concentration and focus. By standing on one foot and maintaining balance, it helps in grounding and stabilizing the mind, which can be particularly beneficial for those with ADHD.

2. **Downward-Facing Dog (Adho Mukha Svanasana)**: This pose is a mild inversion that helps calm the brain and relieve stress. It also energizes the body, which can be helpful for managing hyperactivity.

3. **Warrior II (Virabhadrasana II)**: This pose strengthens focus and concentration. It also helps in building stamina and resilience, teaching individuals to stay present and engaged.

4. **Child's Pose (Balasana)**: Known for its restorative and relaxing qualities, Child's Pose helps in calming the mind and easing stress. It's a good pose for moments of overwhelm or overstimulation.

5. **Corpse Pose (Savasana)**: Though it appears simple, Savasana is a powerful pose for deep relaxation and stress relief. It teaches body awareness and mindfulness, helping individuals with ADHD to quieten their minds.

6. **Eagle Pose (Garudasana)**: This pose requires focus and balance, helping to improve concentration. It also helps in releasing tension in the shoulders and hips, areas where stress is often held.

7. **Cat-Cow Stretch (Marjaryasana-Bitilasana)**: This gentle flow between two poses improves focus and attention to the body. It also helps in soothing and calming the mind, making it ideal for ADHD management.

8. **Cobra Pose (Bhujangasana)**: This backbend stimulates the brain and helps to increase alertness and reduce fatigue. It's also beneficial for strengthening the spine and opening the chest, promoting better breathing.

9. **Butterfly Pose (Baddha Konasana)**: This seated pose is calming and helps in reducing anxiety. It's also good for opening up the hips, where stress and tension can accumulate.

10. *Mountain Pose (Tadasana)*: This foundational pose helps in improving posture, balance, and calmness. It teaches grounding and can be a starting point for mindfulness and presence in the moment.

These poses, when practiced regularly, can offer significant benefits for individuals with ADHD, aiding in better self-regulation, focus, and overall mental well-being. However, it's important to approach yoga practice with patience and consistency to experience these benefits fully.

Pranayama Breathing Techniques

Pranayama is a set of yoga breathing exercises designed to free the flow of prana, or life energy, throughout the body. The practice is crucial because breath is the constant element in our lives, and daily stressors can lead to shallow or stilted breathing patterns. Pranayama aims to energize, relax, and heal the body by balancing this life energy. It involves various techniques that utilize and strengthen different parts of our respiratory system. These techniques can also impact our emotional states, either calming or energizing us. It is recommended to practice pranayama in the morning on an empty stomach.

The Importance of Breath

Breathing is a fundamental aspect of life that often goes unnoticed because it's an automatic process. Our physical and mental health can be greatly impacted by the way we breathe. Here's why the breath is so important:

Physical Health
1. <u>Oxygen Supply</u>: Breathing is the primary way our bodies take in oxygen, which is essential for cellular respiration and energy production.
2. <u>Detoxification</u>: Exhalation helps to remove waste products like carbon dioxide from the body.
3. <u>Cardiovascular Health</u>: Regulating blood pressure and heart rate can be achieved through proper breathing, which contributes to cardiovascular health.

4. <u>Stress Response</u>: The parasympathetic nervous system is activated when you breathe deeply and slowly, which aids in balancing the body's stress response.

Mental Health
1. <u>Focus and Concentration</u>: Mindful breathing can improve focus and concentration by bringing attention to the present moment.
2. <u>Emotional Regulation</u>: Breathing techniques can help manage emotional states, lowering symptoms of anxiety and depression.
3. <u>Mindfulness</u>: Focusing on the breath is a common mindfulness practice that can help you become aware of your thoughts and feelings.

Spiritual Aspect
1. <u>Life Force</u>: In many spiritual traditions, breath is considered the life force or "prana" that connects us to the universal energy.
2. <u>Meditative Practices</u>: Breath is often the focal point in various forms of meditation, helping to achieve a state of inner peace and enlightenment.

Practical Applications
1. <u>Exercise</u>: Proper breathing techniques can enhance athletic performance.
2. <u>Speech and Singing</u>: Breath control is crucial for effective public speaking and singing.
3. <u>Health Interventions</u>: Breathing exercises are often part of therapies for conditions like asthma, COPD, and even some cardiac rehabilitation programs.

Understanding the importance of breath can open doors to improved health, emotional balance, and even spiritual growth. It's a simple yet powerful tool that's always accessible to us.

Mindfulness Techniques

1. ***Body Scan Meditation***: By mentally scanning your body from head to toe, you can observe sensations and release tension.
2. ***Breathing Exercises***: Focusing on your breath can assist you in recognizing the present moment.

3. *Mindful Eating*: The process of eating involves taking your time and savoring each bite, as well as being fully present during meals.
4. *Walking Meditation*: This is a form of meditation in action, where you focus on your steps and your connection with the Earth.
5. *Observation Exercise*: Choose an object and focus all your attention on it for a few minutes, noting its shape, color, texture, and other attributes.

Emotional Freedom Technique (EFT)

1. *Identify the Issue*: The first step in EFT is to identify the emotional or physical issue that you want to address.
2. *Test the Initial Intensity*: Before you begin, assess the intensity of your distress on a scale of 0 to 10.
3. *The Setup*: Tap the "karate chop" point on your hand while affirming something related to your issue.
4. *Tapping Sequence*: Tap on specific points on your body while saying phrases that relate to your issue. The tapping spots commonly occur at the top of the head, eyebrow, side of the eye, under the eye, under the nose, chin, collarbone, and under the arm.
5. *Reassess Intensity*: After a round of tapping, reassess the intensity of your distress. Repeat the process until you feel relief.
6. *Positive Affirmation*: End the session by focusing on a positive affirmation to instill a sense of peace and relaxation.

Both Mindfulness and EFT are techniques that can be self-taught, but they are also often more effective when guided by a trained professional, especially when dealing with more severe emotional or physical issues.

Schedule Problem Solving

Here's a table that outlines some of the challenges mentioned in the journal entry, along with potential solutions and resources that could help a woman navigate life with ADHD.

Challenges	Potential Solutions	Resources
Difficulty focusing at work	Time-blocking, Pomodoro Technique, noise-cancelling headphones	Time management apps, ADHD coaching
Emotional regulation	Mindfulness techniques, Emotional Freedom Technique (EFT)	Mindfulness apps, Therapy
Household tasks	Chore chart, setting reminders	Chore chart apps, Family meetings
Relationship struggles	Open communication, scheduled quality time	Couples therapy, Relationship books
Social life issues	Honest conversations with friends, setting reminders for social events	Social skills workshops, Friendship apps
Overwhelm with simple tasks	Task decomposition, prioritization	Task management apps, ADHD support groups
Feeling misunderstood	Educating close ones about ADHD, seeking a support network	ADHD awareness books, Online ADHD communities
Fear of seeking help	Start with small steps like online research, then move to professional help	Online articles, Therapists specializing in ADHD
Self-esteem issues	Positive affirmations, celebrate small wins	Self-help books, Self-esteem workshops

This table is just a starting point and can be customized further to fit individual needs. It's always logical to ask with healthcare providers for a comprehensive treatment plan.

Relationships: Navigating Love and Friendships

Navigating relationships

It is a complex endeavor for anyone, but for women with ADHD, it can be particularly challenging. The impulsivity, forgetfulness, and emotional dysregulation that often accompany ADHD can strain relationships, whether romantic or platonic. This section aims to provide a comprehensive guide to understanding how ADHD affects relationships and offers actionable advice to manage these challenges effectively.

> ### *Romantic Relationships*

Women with ADHD may find it difficult to maintain romantic relationships due to various factors such as impulsivity, which can lead to hasty decisions like rushing into commitments. Emotional dysregulation can also result in mood swings, causing conflicts and misunderstandings.

- ### *Tools & Techniques*:

- <u>Open Communication</u>: Establish a habit of open and frank communication with your partner.
- <u>Scheduled Check-ins</u>: Regularly set aside time to discuss the relationship and any concerns.

> ### Friendships

Maintaining friendships can also be a struggle. Forgetfulness may lead to missed social events or birthdays, which friends might interpret as a lack of interest or care.

- ### *Tools & Techniques*:

- <u>Digital Reminders</u>: Use calendar apps to set reminders for important dates like birthdays or anniversaries.
- <u>Active Listening</u>: Practice being fully present during conversations to build stronger connections.

> ### Family Relationships

Family dynamics can be complicated by ADHD symptoms. Emotional outbursts can create tension, and impulsivity can lead to conflicts.

- **_Tools & Techniques_**:
- <u>Boundaries</u>: Establish clear boundaries and communicate them effectively to family members.
- <u>Conflict Resolution</u>: Learn techniques to resolve conflicts amicably, such as taking a 'time-out' during heated moments.

➢ **Social Skills**

Women with ADHD often feel socially awkward, which can lead to anxiety in social settings. Feelings of isolation can be further worsened by withdrawing from social activities.

- **_Tools & Techniques_**:
- <u>Social Skills Training</u>: Consider workshops or coaching to improve social skills.
- <u>Mindfulness</u>: Practice mindfulness techniques to manage social anxiety.

➢ **Emotional Intimacy**

Building emotional intimacy can be challenging due to emotional dysregulation. The ups and downs can make it hard to create a stable emotional environment for a relationship to flourish.

- **_Tools & Techniques_**:
- <u>Emotional Journaling</u>: Keep a journal to track your emotional triggers and patterns.
- <u>Therapy</u>: Couples or individual therapy can provide professional guidance.

By addressing these aspects, this section aims to offer a roadmap for women with ADHD to navigate the complex landscape of relationships, armed with practical tools and insights.

ADHD and Sexuality

ADHD can indeed impact various aspects of life, including sexual relationships. The challenges described in your text highlight how ADHD symptoms can interfere with intimacy and sexual satisfaction. Here are some key points and solutions based on the information provided:

Challenges in ADHD and Sexual Intimacy:

1. <u>Difficulty Focusing</u>: ADHD can make it hard to stay mentally present during sex, leading to a lack of emotional intimacy.

2. <u>Need for Excitement</u>: Individuals with ADHD often seek new and exciting experiences, which can lead to boredom in long-term sexual relationships.

3. <u>Power Dynamics</u>: The non-ADHD partner may take on a dominant role in managing household tasks, leading to resentment and a parent-child dynamic rather than a partnership.

4. <u>Time Management Issues</u>: Poor scheduling or time awareness can lead to missed opportunities for intimacy.

Solutions for Enhancing Intimacy:

1. <u>Physical Connection</u>: Simple gestures like holding hands, hugging, or giving massages can strengthen physical and emotional bonds.

2. <u>Regular Dates</u>: Setting aside dedicated time for each other, even if it's just a few minutes each day, can help maintain a romantic connection.

3. <u>Romantic Gestures</u>: Small acts like leaving love notes can remind your partner of your affection and commitment.

Additional Strategies:

- <u>Practice Lingering</u>: Those with ADHD can practice staying engaged in the moment in non-sexual settings to improve focus during intimate moments.

- <u>Rebalance the Relationship</u>: Sharing responsibilities more equally can help alleviate the parent-child dynamic, fostering a more equal and romantic partnership.

- <u>Seek Therapy</u>: A skilled therapist can provide tailored strategies to address ADHD-related challenges in relationships.

Understanding ADHD's Role:

- <u>Biological vs. Emotional</u>: Recognizing that ADHD symptoms are often biological rather than emotional can help couples understand and address the root causes of intimacy issues.

Understanding and addressing the unique challenges that ADHD presents in sexual relationships is crucial. By focusing on physical connection, dedicated time, and romantic gestures, couples can enhance intimacy. Additionally, rebalancing relationship dynamics and seeking professional help can provide further support. It's important to remember that these challenges are often due to ADHD symptoms and not a lack of love or commitment.

Date: October 21, 2023

Dear Diary

(Today was tough) The conversation with Mark last night left a crater in my chest. I feel like I'm constantly disappointing him because my mind works differently. I could see the frustration in his eyes when I forgot about our dinner plans, again. It wasn't the first time, and I hate that my forgetfulness is becoming a pattern that's hard to break.

(Frustrations) I want to be present in this relationship, I want to remember the little things and the big plans. Each time I forget, I see a little more disappointment in his eyes. Today, I tried to talk to him about it, but the words got tangled up and nothing came out right. I hate how my ADHD makes simple conversations feel like navigating through a labyrinth.

(Fears) I'm terrified that one day, he'll decide that loving me is too complicated. That the chaos in my mind is too much to handle. What if my struggles with ADHD become the obstacle that causes us to fall apart? I love him so much, but sometimes I fear that my ADHD is a burden he didn't sign up for.

(Demotivation and Hopelessness) It feels like a dark cloud is hanging over me. The harder I try to overcome my symptoms, the more hopeless I feel. There's a voice inside me that keeps whispering that I'm not good enough, not for him, not for anyone. I wish I could silence it, but it's loud today.

(Insecurities) My insecurities are like a monster lurking in the shadows. They catch me off guard when I least expect it. Today, they're roaring loud, telling me that I'll never be able to provide Mark with the stability he deserves. I wish I could be different, be better for him.

(Seeking Comfort) I sat by the window, watching the rain pour down, hoping it would wash away the heaviness in my heart. I wish I had answers, a way to make things right. For now, all I can do is write down these swirling thoughts, hoping to find some clarity amidst the storm inside me.

Title: Whirlwind of Emotions

This journal entry aims to capture the emotional turmoil and reflections of a woman with ADHD navigating a challenging day in her relationship. Through her words, she conveys her frustrations, fears, feelings of demotivation, and insecurities, while also seeking a sense of solace and understanding through journaling.

Research Problem Solving: Taking matters into your own hands.

Given the emotional struggles and challenges in the relationship as described in the previous journal entry, here's a structured plan to address and work through these issues:

Problem-Solving Plan: October 22, 2023
1. *Identify the Problems*:
 - Forgetfulness leading to missed plans and disappointments.
 - Difficulty in communicating feelings and thoughts effectively.
 - Fear of the relationship becoming strained due to ADHD symptoms.

2. Set Specific Goals:
 - Improve memory and organization to remember plans and commitments.
 - Enhance communication within the relationship.
 - Foster understanding and support regarding ADHD in the relationship.

3. Develop Strategies:
 - *For Improving Memory and Organization*:
 - Use digital calendars and reminders for all plans and appointments.
 - Create a visible daily schedule to keep track of tasks and commitments.
 - Incorporate mindfulness practices to enhance present-moment awareness.

 - *For Enhancing Communication*:
 - Schedule regular check-in conversations to discuss feelings, concerns, and plans.

- Consider attending couples' counseling to improve communication skills.
- Practice expressing thoughts and feelings through writing before discussing them verbally.

- *For Fostering Understanding and Support*:
- Share resources and information about ADHD with the partner to foster understanding.
- Attend ADHD support groups or counseling together to learn coping strategies.
- Be open about challenges and seek support from each other in overcoming them.

4. Implement the Plan:

- Start implementing these strategies on a daily basis.
- Keep a progress journal to monitor improvements and challenges.
- Communicate openly with the partner about the progress and any adjustments needed in the strategies.

5. Evaluate the Plan:

- After a month, evaluate the effectiveness of the strategies implemented.
- Discuss with the partner about what has improved and what still needs work.
- Adjust the plan as necessary based on feedback and experiences.

6. Seek Professional Help if Necessary:

- If challenges persist, consider seeking professional help such as couples counseling or individual therapy for further support and guidance.

This plan is designed to provide a structured approach to addressing the identified problems, setting clear goals, and developing actionable strategies. Through implementation, evaluation, and adjustment of the plan, the aim is to work towards improving the relationship and managing ADHD symptoms in a supportive and understanding environment.

Weekly Schedule

Day	Time	Activity Type	Description	Location	Notes
Monday	7:00-8:00	Family Dinner	A sit-down dinner to catch up on everyone's day	Home	Screen-free time
Tuesday	6:30-7:30	Exercise Time	Family yoga or a walk in the park	Local Park	Bring water bottles
Wednesday	8:00-9:00	Date Night	Dinner at a quiet restaurant	Local Restaurant	Make reservations in advance
Thursday	7:30-8:30	Creative Time	Painting or crafting with the kids	Home	Prepare materials beforehand
Friday	6:00-8:00	Movie Night	Family movie night with popcorn	Home	Pick a movie everyone enjoys
Saturday	10:00-12:00	Outdoor Adventure	Hiking, biking, or a day at the beach	Various Locations	Pack snacks and sunscreen
Sunday	9:00-10:00	Planning & Reflection	Discuss the week ahead and any special events	Home	Use a family calendar

Monthly Schedule

Date	Time	Activity Type	Description	Location	Notes
1st Sunday	4:00-6:00	Family Game Day	Board games and snacks	Home	Rotate who picks the games
2nd Friday	7:00-9:00	Romantic Date Night	A special outing just for the couple	Various Locations	Alternate planning responsibility
3rd Saturday	11:00-2:00	Picnic & Park Day	A picnic lunch and playtime at the park	Local Park	Bring a frisbee or ball
Last Sunday	5:00-7:00	Monthly Reflection	Discuss the highs and lows of the month	Home	Prepare for the month ahead

Notes:

- The schedule is designed to be flexible and can be adjusted based on specific needs and commitments.
- Activities are chosen to be engaging but not overly stimulating, considering the ADHD factor.
- "Planning & Reflection" time on Sundays can be used to adjust the schedule as needed.

This schedule aims to provide a balanced mix of family time, couple time, and individual time, taking into consideration the unique challenges faced by women with ADHD. It's important to stick to the schedule as much as possible but also to allow for flexibility when needed.

Parenting with ADHD: Tips for Moms

Parenting is a challenging task, and when you add ADHD into the mix, it can become even more complex. However, it's important to remember that having ADHD doesn't make you a less capable parent; it just means you may need to approach things a bit differently. Here's a bullet point that encapsulates some key tips for moms who are parenting with ADHD:

Parenting with ADHD: Tips for Moms

- ***Structure and Routine***: Create a daily routine to help both you and your children know what to expect. This can be especially helpful in managing ADHD symptoms.
- ***Time Management***: Use timers, alarms, and calendars to help you manage your time effectively. Consider a specialized calendar tailored for ADHD to help you prioritize tasks.
- ***Self-Care***: Don't forget to take time for yourself. Exercise, meditate, or engage in activities that help you relax and recharge.
- ***Be Present***: ADHD can make it challenging to focus. Try mindfulness techniques to help you be present in the moment with your children.
- ***Seek Support***: Whether it's from family, friends, or support groups, don't hesitate to ask for help. You don't have to go it alone.
- ***Open Communication***: Be open with your children about your ADHD. This can help them understand why mom might do things a little differently and can also destigmatize ADHD.
- ***Celebrate Small Wins***: Parenting is filled with challenges. Celebrate the small victories to keep yourself motivated.
- ***Use Technology***: There are various apps and tools designed to help with task management and reminders. Utilize these to make your daily tasks easier.
- ***Be Kind to Yourself***: Parenting is hard, and it's okay to make mistakes. Learn from them and move on, rather than dwelling on them.

By incorporating these tips into your daily life, you can create a more harmonious and effective parenting strategy that works for you and your family.

The Workplace: Achieving Success in Your Career

Navigating the workplace can be a complex endeavor, especially for individuals with ADHD. However, with the right strategies and tools, achieving success in your career is entirely possible. Here's a bullet point that outlines some key tips for thriving in the workplace:

The Workplace: Achieving Success in Your Career

- ***Prioritize Tasks***: Use tools like to-do lists or specialized ADHD-friendly calendars to help you prioritize your tasks based on urgency and importance.
    - **How**: Use Eisenhower's Urgent-Important Matrix to categorize tasks.
    - **Why**: This helps you focus on what truly matters, reducing the stress of having to juggle multiple tasks at once.

- ***Time Management***: Utilize time management techniques such as the Pomodoro Technique or time-blocking to help you focus on tasks for specific periods.
    - **How**: Techniques like the Pomodoro Technique involve working in bursts of focused time (usually 25 minutes) followed by short breaks.
    - **Why**: This can help you maintain focus and productivity without feeling overwhelmed.

- ***Set Boundaries***: Make it clear when you are available for meetings or socializing and when you need to focus on work. Use physical or digital "Do Not Disturb" signs if necessary.
    - **How**: Clearly communicate your working hours and break times to colleagues.
    - **Why**: This ensures that you have uninterrupted time to focus on tasks, making you more efficient.

- ***Organize Your Workspace***: A clutter-free and organized workspace can help reduce distractions and increase productivity. Consider using organizers, labels, and digital tools to keep everything in its place.
    - **How**: Use physical organizers for paperwork and digital tools for computer files.

- **Why**: A clean workspace minimizes distractions and makes it easier to find what you need, saving time and reducing stress.

- **_Take Breaks_**: Short breaks can help you recharge and improve focus. Use this time to stretch, take a walk, or engage in a quick mindfulness exercise.
  - **How**: Short breaks like a 5-minute walk or some light stretching can be beneficial.
  - **Why**: Breaks can help reset your focus and reduce the risk of burnout.

- **_Seek Accommodations_**: If your ADHD symptoms significantly impact your work, consider talking to HR about possible accommodations, such as a quieter workspace or flexible hours.
  - **How**: Discuss your needs with Human Resources for possible accommodations like noise-cancelling headphones or a more secluded workspace.
  - **Why**: Tailoring your work environment to suit your needs can significantly improve productivity and job satisfaction.

- **_Professional Development_**: Invest in yourself by taking courses, attending workshops, or seeking mentorship to improve your skills and stay updated in your field.
  - **How**: Take online courses, attend seminars, or read industry-related materials.
  - **Why**: Continuous learning keeps you competitive and can open doors to new opportunities.

- **_Network Effectively:_** Building a strong professional network can open doors to new opportunities. Attend industry events, join professional organizations, and maintain your LinkedIn profile.
  - **How**: Attend industry events, engage on professional social media, and don't hesitate to reach out to people in your field.
  - **Why**: Networking can provide you with valuable insights and can be a source of job opportunities.

- **_Be Open to Feedback_**: Constructive criticism is a part of any job. Learn to accept feedback gracefully and use it as an opportunity for growth.

- **How**: Listen actively to feedback, ask for clarification if needed, and create an action plan for improvement.
- **Why**: Constructive criticism is an opportunity for growth and improvement.

- **_Celebrate Achievements_**: Whether it's completing a challenging project or receiving a promotion, take the time to celebrate your achievements, no matter how small.
- **How**: Take a moment to acknowledge your hard work, whether it's by treating yourself to something nice or simply taking a moment to reflect.
- **Why**: Celebrating achievements, no matter how small, boosts your morale and motivation.

By implementing these strategies, you can create a work environment that not only accommodates your ADHD but also allows you to excel in your career.

Part IV: Emotional Well-being

Emotional well-being is a critical yet often overlooked aspect of living with ADHD. While much attention is given to managing symptoms that affect focus and productivity, emotional regulation is equally important. ADHD can sometimes exacerbate feelings of frustration, impulsivity, and emotional sensitivity, making it challenging to navigate both personal and professional relationships. This chapter aims to provide a comprehensive guide to understanding and improving your emotional well-being while living with ADHD.

Firstly, it's essential to recognize that emotional dysregulation is not a sign of weakness or a lack of discipline. It's a common experience for many individuals with ADHD and is rooted in neurobiological factors. Understanding this can alleviate some of the guilt or shame that often accompanies emotional struggles, making it easier to seek appropriate help.

Mindfulness techniques can be particularly effective in improving emotional well-being. Practices such as deep breathing, meditation, and grounding exercises can help you become aware of your emotional state, giving you the space to choose how to respond rather than react impulsively. These techniques can be easily incorporated into your daily routine and can provide immediate relief in emotionally charged situations.

Another crucial aspect is the role of social support. Emotional well-being is significantly influenced by the quality of your relationships. Surrounding yourself with understanding and supportive individuals can provide a safety net for when you're struggling. Support groups, either in person or online, can also offer invaluable insights and coping strategies from people who are going through similar experiences.

Lastly, professional help should never be underestimated. Counselors and counselors trained in ADHD can provide targeted cognitive-behavioral strategies to improve emotional regulation. Medication can also be an option for some, serving as a complementary approach to behavioral strategies.

In summary, emotional well-being is an integral part of managing ADHD. By adopting mindfulness techniques, seeking social support, and considering professional help, you can create a holistic approach to improve not just your focus and productivity, but also your emotional health. This chapter aims to be a resource that empowers you to take control of your emotional well-being, thereby improving your overall quality of life.

Self-Esteem and Self-Compassion: Loving Yourself

Self-esteem and self-compassion are foundational elements of emotional well-being, especially for individuals with ADHD who may often find themselves grappling with feelings of inadequacy or self-doubt. While self-esteem focuses on the evaluation of one's worth, self-compassion emphasizes treating oneself with the same kindness and understanding as one would offer a good friend. Together, these two concepts form a powerful duo for enhancing emotional health.

Why It's Important

Low self-esteem can exacerbate ADHD symptoms by creating a cycle of negative self-talk and avoidance behavior. This can lead to procrastination, poor performance, and ultimately, a further decline in self-esteem. Self-compassion, on the other hand, allows for an emotional "reset," offering a kinder perspective that acknowledges imperfections as a natural part of the human experience.

Practical Steps

1. *Positive Affirmations*: Start your day with positive affirmations that reinforce your worth and capabilities.
2. *Mindfulness Meditation*: Engage in mindfulness practices that focus on self-love and acceptance.
3. *Journaling*: Keep a journal to track your thoughts and feelings, making it easier to identify patterns of negative self-talk that you can work on changing.
4. *Set Achievable Goals*: Break down tasks into smaller, manageable goals and celebrate your achievements, no matter how minor they may seem.

The Role of Self-Compassion

Self-compassion involves three key elements: self-kindness, common humanity, and mindfulness. Self-kindness encourages you to be understanding toward yourself when you fail or make mistakes. Common humanity reminds you that you're not alone in your struggles, and mindfulness allows you to observe your thoughts and feelings without judgment.

Combining Self-Esteem and Self-Compassion
By combining a healthy level of self-esteem with the nurturing quality of self-compassion, you create a balanced emotional state that is resilient to life's ups and downs. This doesn't mean you won't face challenges or difficulties, but it equips you with the emotional tools to handle them more effectively.

In summary, self-esteem and self-compassion are not just buzzwords; they are essential components of emotional well-being. By actively practicing these principles, you can significantly improve your emotional resilience, your relationships, and your overall quality of life.

<u>*Example of Emotional Journal*</u>

Journal Entry: October 3, 2023

Dear Journal,
Today was another one of those days where I felt like I was drowning in a sea of expectations, judgments, and misunderstandings. I woke up with the best intentions, really. I had my to-do list ready, my alarms set, and my mind focused—or at least, I tried to make it so. But as the day unfolded, so did my emotional state.

At work, I felt like an alien in a world where everyone else seemed to have it together. My colleagues managed their tasks effortlessly, while I struggled to keep my focus for more than 10 minutes. I could feel their eyes on me, silently questioning my capabilities. "Why is she so disorganized?" They must be thinking. "Why can't she just get it together?" And the worst part is, I ask myself the same questions.

I've read all the self-help books, listened to all the podcasts, and even attended wellness retreats. But here I am, still unable to regulate my emotions or manage my time effectively. It's like I'm in a constant battle with myself, and I'm losing.

When I got home, I thought I could find some solace, but family life is another battlefield. My husband doesn't understand why simple tasks seem so overwhelming to me. "Why is the laundry still not done?" he asked, not knowing that his simple question felt like an attack on my already fragile self-esteem. I want to be the wife who has it all together, but most days, I feel like I'm falling apart.

And then there's my social life, or lack thereof. My friends have stopped inviting me to gatherings, probably tired of my last-minute cancellations or forgetfulness. I don't blame them. Who would want to be friends with someone so unreliable? But what they don't understand is that it's not intentional. My mind is like a browser with too many tabs open, and I can't seem to find the one that plays the annoying music.

I feel so isolated, like I'm living in a bubble that no one else can see or understand. People think ADHD is just about being hyper or easily distracted, but it's so much more than that. It's about feeling so overwhelmed by the simplest tasks that you end up doing nothing. It's about wanting to have meaningful relationships but sabotaging them because you can't keep up with social norms. It's about feeling so much all the time that you end up feeling nothing at all.

I'm tired, Journal. I'm tired of feeling misunderstood, of constantly having to explain myself, of feeling like a failure in every aspect of my life. I'm tired of the judgment, the shame, and the never-ending cycle of hopelessness.

I know I need help, but the thought of seeking it is another task on my never-ending list of things to do. And what if it doesn't work? What if I'm just destined to live my life in this chaotic state of mind? That's my biggest fear: that no matter what I do, I'll always be this version of myself.

But tomorrow is another day, and maybe, just maybe, it'll be the day I find the strength to break this cycle. Until then, all I have are these pages to confide in, the only place where I don't feel judged or misunderstood. Here's to hoping for a better tomorrow.

Sincerely,

A Woman Trying to Navigate Life with ADHD.

Schedule Problem Solving

Here's a table that outlines some of the challenges mentioned in the journal entry, along with potential solutions and resources that could help a woman navigate life with ADHD.

Challenges	Potential Solutions	Resources
Difficulty focusing at work	Time-blocking, Pomodoro Technique, noise-cancelling headphones	Time management apps, ADHD coaching
Emotional regulation	Mindfulness techniques, Emotional Freedom Technique (EFT)	Mindfulness apps, Therapy
Household tasks	Chore chart, setting reminders	Chore chart apps, Family meetings
Relationship struggles	Open communication, scheduled quality time	Couples therapy, Relationship books
Social life issues	Honest conversations with friends, setting reminders for social events	Social skills workshops, Friendship apps
Overwhelm with simple tasks	Task decomposition, prioritization	Task management apps, ADHD support groups
Feeling misunderstood	Educating close ones about ADHD, seeking a support network	ADHD awareness books, Online ADHD communities
Fear of seeking help	Start with small steps like online research, then move to professional help	Online articles, Therapists specializing in ADHD
Self-esteem issues	Positive affirmations, celebrate small wins	Self-help books, Self-esteem workshops

This table is just a starting point and can be customized further to fit individual needs. It's always advisable to consult with healthcare providers for a comprehensive treatment plan.

Coping with Rejection Sensitive Dysphoria

Rejection Sensitive Dysphoria (RSD) is an emotional condition often associated with ADHD, characterized by extreme emotional sensitivity and emotional pain. It can manifest as an overwhelming fear of rejection or criticism, even if such rejection or criticism is either imagined or relatively minor. Coping with RSD can be a complex process, but there are several strategies that can help manage its symptoms:

1. Cognitive Behavioral Therapy (CBT): This form of therapy can help individuals understand the patterns and beliefs that lead to RSD. By identifying these triggers, one can learn to manage their emotional reactions better.

2. Medication: Antidepressants and anti-anxiety medications can sometimes help manage the symptoms of RSD. Always consult a healthcare provider for a diagnosis and treatment plan tailored to your needs.

3. Mindfulness Techniques: Mindfulness can help individuals become aware of their thoughts and feelings and make it easier to control their emotional reactions to perceived rejections or criticisms.

4. Social Support: Having a strong support system can be invaluable in coping with RSD. Trusted friends and family can offer emotional support and validation, which can be incredibly healing.

5. Self-Compassion: Learning to be kinder to oneself can help manage the symptoms of RSD. Self-compassion exercises can help you learn to be less critical of yourself, thereby reducing the emotional pain associated with perceived rejections.

6. Setting Boundaries: Learning to set emotional and physical boundaries can help protect against the emotional turmoil that can come from perceived rejections or criticisms.

7. Professional Help: Sometimes, the symptoms of RSD can be too overwhelming to manage alone. In such cases, seeking the help of a psychologist or psychiatrist can provide additional coping strategies.

8. Education and Awareness: Understanding the nature of RSD can itself be a powerful tool. The more you know about what you're experiencing, the less frightening those experiences become.

9. Positive Affirmations: Repeating positive affirmations can help rewire the brain to react less severely to triggers that might cause an RSD episode.

10. <u>Physical Exercise</u>: Physical activities like jogging, swimming, or even a simple walk can release endorphins, which are natural mood lifters. They can help in reducing the severity of RSD symptoms.

By incorporating these strategies into your life, you can develop a comprehensive approach to managing RSD. It's often beneficial to consult with healthcare providers for a tailored treatment plan that's appropriate for you.

Managing Emotional Overwhelm

Managing Emotional Overwhelm is a crucial topic that addresses the heightened emotional states often experienced by individuals, particularly those with ADHD. Emotional overwhelm can manifest in various ways, including anxiety, frustration, or even a sense of paralysis when faced with tasks or social situations. This emotional turbulence is not just a fleeting feeling but can significantly impact one's ability to function effectively in daily life.

The section on Managing Emotional Overwhelm aims to provide readers with practical tools and strategies to navigate these intense emotional landscapes. It delves into the underlying causes of emotional overwhelm, such as sensory overload, lack of emotional regulation skills, or the presence of co-existing mental health conditions like anxiety or depression. Understanding the root causes is the first step in developing coping mechanisms.

The chapter offers actionable tips like mindfulness techniques, grounding exercises, and cognitive behavioral strategies to manage emotional spikes. It also emphasizes the importance of self-compassion and self-awareness, encouraging readers to take a step back and assess their emotional state objectively rather than spiraling further into overwhelm.

Moreover, the section may include real-life case studies to illustrate how individuals have successfully managed emotional overwhelm in various scenarios. These narratives serve both as educational tools and sources of inspiration for readers who may be struggling with similar issues.

By addressing Managing Emotional Overwhelm, the book aims to equip readers with the emotional resilience and psychological tools necessary to improve their quality of life. It's not just about surviving emotional overwhelm but thriving despite it.

Tool & Strategies

Navigating intense emotional landscapes requires a multi-faceted approach that combines various practical tools and strategies. Here's a detailed look at some of the actionable tips mentioned:

Mindfulness Techniques

Mindfulness is the practice of being fully present and engaged in the moment, aware of your thoughts and feelings without judgment. This can be particularly useful for managing sensory overload, a common trigger for emotional overwhelm.

- *Breathing Exercises*: Focusing on your breath can help you become aware of your thoughts and feelings. Try the 4-7-8 technique: inhale through the nose for 4 seconds, hold the breath for 7 seconds, and exhale through the mouth for 8 seconds.

- *Body Scan*: This involves mentally scanning your body from head to toe, observing sensations, and releasing tension. It helps you become aware of physical sensations that accompany emotional overwhelm.

Grounding Exercises

Grounding exercises can help you divert your focus from emotional or mental stress to physical sensations. These are particularly useful for those who lack emotional regulation skills.

- *5-4-3-2-1 Method*: Identify 5 things you can see, 4 things you can touch, 3 things you can hear, 2 things you can smell, and 1 thing you can taste. This exercise helps you become aware of your surroundings and diverts your attention from emotional or mental distress.

- *Physical Grounding*: This could be as simple as feeling your feet on the ground or holding onto a familiar object. The tactile sensations serve as a reminder that you are here and now, not in the imagined scenarios causing stress.

Cognitive Behavioral Strategies

Cognitive Behavioral Therapy (CBT) techniques can be effective in changing the thought patterns that contribute to emotional overwhelm.

- *Thought Journaling*: Keep a journal where you write down situations that trigger emotional overwhelm, the thoughts that went through your mind, and how you reacted. This helps in identifying negative thought patterns and irrational beliefs.
- *Reframing*: This involves challenging your negative thoughts and beliefs and replacing them with more positive or realistic

ones. For example, instead of thinking, "*I can't handle this*," you might reframe it to, "I can *take this one step at a time.*"

- *Problem-Solving*: Instead of ruminating on your issues, focus on potential solutions. Break down the problem into smaller, manageable tasks and tackle them one at a time.

By integrating these mindfulness techniques, grounding exercises, and cognitive behavioral strategies into your daily routine, you can better manage emotional overwhelm. These tools not only help in the moment but also build emotional resilience over time.

The Importance of a Support Network

"The Importance of a Support Network" delves into the critical role that a reliable and understanding circle of friends, family, and professionals can play in the life of someone with ADHD. Living with ADHD often comes with challenges that can be overwhelming to navigate alone. A support network serves as a safety net, offering emotional support, practical advice, and sometimes even professional guidance.

Firstly, emotional support is invaluable for anyone, but for someone with ADHD, it can be a lifeline. The condition often comes with emotional dysregulation, making it difficult to manage feelings of frustration, disappointment, or anxiety. A supportive network can offer a listening ear, validation, and emotional comfort.

Secondly, practical advice from those who have either lived with ADHD or have expertise in the area can offer actionable steps for daily challenges. Whether it's advice on managing time, staying organized, or even tips on medication and alternative treatments, a support network can provide a wealth of information.

Thirdly, a professional support network, including doctors, therapists, and counselors, can offer medical and psychological interventions. They can help with diagnosis, medication management, and provide cognitive behavioral therapy or other forms of treatment.

Moreover, a support network can also serve as accountability partners. Whether it's a friend who checks in on your well-being or a family member who helps you stay on track with your medication, these individuals can offer the kind of accountability that is often needed when living with ADHD.

Lastly, a support network provides a sense of belonging and acceptance. The feeling of being understood and not judged for the challenges that come with ADHD is empowering. It can significantly improve self-esteem and provide the emotional strength needed to face daily challenges.

In summary, a support network is not just beneficial but essential for individuals with ADHD. It offers emotional sustenance, practical advice, professional guidance, accountability, and a sense of belonging, making it easier to navigate the complexities of life with ADHD.

Part V: Problem Solving and Proven Strategies

This chapter serves as a comprehensive guide to tackling some of the most challenging aspects of living with ADHD. It is designed to equip you with actionable strategies and tools for better financial planning, decision-making, and goal setting. It is particularly crucial because these areas often pose significant difficulties for individuals with ADHD due to issues like impulsivity, poor time management, and difficulty in prioritizing tasks.

Firstly, the section on _"Financial Planning"_ delves into the unique challenges that ADHD individuals face when it comes to managing money. It offers practical advice on budgeting, saving, and investing, tailored to the ADHD brain. The chapter provides tools like budgeting apps designed for ADHD individuals and techniques to automate savings and bill payments, thus reducing the cognitive load and potential for error.

Next, the "_Decision Making_" segment addresses the common ADHD traits of impulsivity and indecisiveness. It introduces proven strategies like the Eisenhower Matrix for urgent vs. important tasks and the Pomodoro Technique for time management. These tools aim to help you make more informed and less impulsive decisions by providing a structured framework to evaluate options and consequences.

Lastly, "_Goal Setting_" is a focal point of this chapter, recognizing that individuals with ADHD often struggle with long-term planning due to their focus on immediate rewards. It introduces the SMART goals framework (Specific, Measurable, Achievable, Relevant, Time-bound) tailored for ADHD. This section also emphasizes the importance of breaking down larger goals into smaller, manageable tasks and using visual aids like vision boards to keep track of progress.

Overall, Part V serves as a toolkit for navigating the complexities of life with ADHD. It combines evidence-based strategies with practical tips, offering a holistic approach to improving financial health, making better decisions, and setting achievable goals. This chapter is an invaluable resource for anyone looking to take control of their life while managing the symptoms of ADHD.

Financial Planning: Budgeting and Avoiding Impulse Spending

Financial planning for individuals with ADHD often requires special attention to budgeting and impulse spending, two areas that can be particularly challenging due to issues with attention and impulsivity.

Budgeting:

Effective budgeting starts with understanding your income and expenses. Apps like YNAB (You Need A Budget) or Mint can be incredibly helpful. These apps categorize your spending and allow you to allocate funds for specific needs, making it easier to stick to your budget. The key is to review your budget regularly, perhaps weekly, to adjust as needed. This frequent check-in can help keep you accountable and aware of your financial situation, which is crucial for those with ADHD who may struggle with forgetfulness or procrastination.

Avoiding Impulse Spending:

Impulse spending can be a significant issue for individuals with ADHD. To combat this, consider implementing a "cooling-off" period for purchases over a certain amount. During this time, evaluate whether the item is a need or a want. Apps like PocketGuard can help by showing you how much 'spendable' money you have left after all essential expenses, making it easier to resist the urge to splurge. Another strategy is to use cash or debit cards instead of credit cards, as physical money tends to feel more 'real,' making you think twice before spending it.

By combining effective budgeting strategies with mechanisms to control impulse spending, you can create a financial planning system that accommodates the unique challenges posed by ADHD.

Examples of Tools and Tips of Financial Planning

Here are some practical tips and tools specifically designed to help individuals with ADHD manage their finances more effectively. Recognizing that impulsivity and poor attention to detail can be significant hurdles, this section aims to simplify the financial planning process and make it more ADHD-friendly.

Budgeting Tools:

1. *YNAB* (You Need A Budget): This app is excellent for those who need to see where every dollar is going. It helps you allocate money for different categories and keeps you accountable.

2. _Mint_: This app automatically categorizes your spending and helps you keep track of bills, budget, and savings. It's a more hands-off approach for those who find budgeting tedious.

3. _PocketGuard_: This app focuses on showing you how much 'spendable' money you have after accounting for bills, savings, and budget items, making it easier to avoid impulsive spending.

Automating Savings:

1. _Twine_: A joint savings app that helps couples save for shared goals. It's excellent for accountability.

2. _Acorns_: This app rounds up your purchases to the nearest dollar and invests the change, making saving almost effortless.

3. _Chime_: An online bank that automatically transfers 10% of every paycheck into a separate savings account.

Bill Payment Techniques:

1. _Auto-Pay_: Most utility and subscription services offer an auto-pay option. Enabling this ensures that you never miss a payment and incur late fees.

2. _Calendar Reminders_: Use digital calendars to set reminders a few days before a bill is due. This is especially useful for bills that can't be automated.

3. _Bill Tracker_: An app that keeps track of all your bills, their due dates, and can even set reminders.

4. _Bank Alerts_: Set up alerts with your bank to notify you when a large transaction occurs, or your balance falls below a certain level, helping you avoid overdraft fees.

ADHD-Specific Tips:

1. _Envelope System_: Physically divide cash for different expenses into separate envelopes. It's an old-school method but effective for those who struggle with digital numbers.

2. _Financial Planner_: Consider hiring a financial planner who has experience working with ADHD clients. They can provide personalized strategies that work for you.

3. _Weekly Check-ins_: Set a specific time each week to review your financial status. Use this time to update your budget, review your accounts, and track your financial goals.

By integrating these apps and techniques into your financial routine, you can create a system that works with your ADHD, not against it, making financial management a less daunting task.

Decision Making: Overcoming Analysis Paralysis

Decision-making can often lead to a state of "analysis paralysis," a condition where overthinking and overanalyzing options result in decision-making inertia. This is especially true for individuals with ADHD, who may already struggle with impulsivity and distractibility. Overcoming analysis paralysis requires a blend of cognitive strategies and practical steps.

- ***Cognitive Reframing***:

Firstly, it's essential to reframe the decision-making process as an opportunity rather than a burden. Understand that not all decisions are life-altering; it's okay to make mistakes. Cognitive Behavioral Therapy (CBT) techniques can help in this reframing process.

- ***Time-Bound Decisions***:

Setting a time limit for making a decision can be incredibly freeing. Use a timer if necessary. The constraint can act as a catalyst, forcing you to prioritize essential factors over trivial ones.

- ***Simplify Choices***:

Too many options can be overwhelming. Narrow down your choices to a manageable number by eliminating less feasible or less attractive alternatives right off the bat.

- **The Two-Minute Rule**:

For smaller decisions, apply the "two-minute rule." If a decision can be made in two minutes or less, make it immediately. This practice helps build decision-making confidence over time.

- ***Mindfulness and Grounding Techniques***:

When you find yourself spiraling into over analysis, grounding techniques such as deep breathing or focusing on sensory experiences can help bring you back to the present moment.

By employing these strategies, you can break free from the shackles of analysis paralysis, making the decision-making process less daunting and more effective.

Also remembering that decision making can be a complex process, it's crucial to have a structured approach to making decisions, both big and small.

Structured Approach:
One effective method is the "***STOP-START-CONTINUE***" framework.
- "<u>*STOP*</u>" and think about the decision at hand.
- "<u>START</u>" gathering information and considering the pros and cons.
- "<u>CONTINUE</u>" to make the decision based on the information and self-reflection you've done. This methodical approach can help slow down the impulsivity often associated with ADHD.

Tools and Techniques:
Apps like "***<u>ChoiceMap</u>***" can help you make decisions by guiding you through a series of questions to evaluate your options objectively. Another tool is the <u>*Eisenhower Matrix (pag.61),*</u> which helps you prioritize tasks based on their urgency and importance. This can be particularly useful for those who struggle with decision-making related to time management.

Emotional Considerations:
People with ADHD often make decisions based on how they feel rather than logical reasoning. Emotional regulation techniques, such as mindfulness and deep-breathing exercises, can help in calming the mind and making more rational decisions.

Consult and Reflect:
It's also beneficial to consult trusted individuals when making significant decisions. Sometimes, just the act of verbalizing your thoughts can provide clarity. After making a decision, reflect on the outcomes to understand what worked and what didn't. This reflection can be a learning experience for future decision-making.

By employing these strategies and tools, individuals with ADHD can improve their decision-making skills, leading to more positive outcomes in various aspects of life.

Goal Setting: Achievable Steps for Long-term Success

Goal setting is a critical skill for long-term success, especially for individuals with ADHD who might struggle with focus, organization, and follow-through. Effective goal setting involves breaking down larger objectives into smaller, achievable steps, allowing for more manageable and realistic progress tracking.

1. ***Define Clear, Specific Goals***:
   - <u>Clarity</u>: Goals should be clear and specific. Instead of "get better at managing time," aim for "spend 30 minutes each day on task management."
   - <u>Measurability</u>: Ensure that your goals are measurable. For instance, if your goal is to save money, specify an amount and timeframe.

2. ***Break Goals into Smaller Tasks***:
   - <u>Task Division</u>: Large goals can be overwhelming. Break them into smaller, actionable tasks to avoid feeling swamped.
   - <u>Prioritization</u>: Prioritize these tasks based on urgency and importance.

3. ***Set Realistic Deadlines***:
   - <u>Time Management</u>: Assign realistic deadlines to each task and overall goal. Consider using a digital calendar or planner to keep track.
   - <u>Flexibility</u>: Be flexible with deadlines, understanding that sometimes adjustments are necessary.

4. ***Use Tools and Resources***:
   - <u>Digital Aids</u>: Utilize apps and tools for reminders and tracking progress. Tools like Trello, Asana, or simple to-do list apps can be effective.
   - <u>Visual Aids</u>: Consider visual aids like mind maps or vision boards to keep goals visible and top of mind.

5. ***Regular Review and Adjustments***:
   - <u>Progress Tracking</u>: Regularly review your progress towards your goals. This can be done weekly or monthly.
   - <u>Adaptability</u>: Be prepared to adjust goals as needed. Flexibility is key to managing any unforeseen challenges.

6. ***Accountability and Support***:
   - <u>Support Networks</u>: Share your goals with a trusted friend, family member, or coach who can provide support and accountability.
   - <u>Self-Compassion</u>: Be kind to yourself. Recognize your efforts and progress, even if things don't always go as planned.

7. ***Celebrate Achievements***:
   - <u>Rewards</u>: Set up a reward system for reaching milestones. This can be as simple as a favorite activity or a small treat.
   - <u>Reflection</u>: Reflect on what you learned during the process and how it can apply to future goals.

By following these steps, individuals with ADHD can create a structured approach to achieving their goals, turning aspirations into tangible successes.

Part VI: Real Stories, Real Women

This chapter would typically feature personal narratives and case studies from various women who live with ADHD. These stories serve multiple purposes:

1. ***Diverse Experiences***:
   - <u>Variety of Backgrounds</u>: Stories from women of different ages, ethnicities, and socio-economic backgrounds.
   - <u>Unique Challenges</u>: Each story highlights individual challenges and experiences, reflecting the diverse ways ADHD can manifest in women.

2. ***Common Struggles***:
   - <u>Shared Difficulties</u>: Despite their differences, these stories often reveal common struggles such as managing daily tasks, dealing with emotional dysregulation, or facing societal misunderstandings about ADHD.

- <u>Coping Mechanisms</u>: Insights into how each woman copes with her symptoms, including both successful strategies and ongoing challenges.

3. *Impact on Life Stages*:
- <u>Different Life Phases</u>: Accounts may cover various life stages, such as adolescence, adulthood, motherhood, and menopause, offering a comprehensive view of how ADHD affects women throughout their lives.
- <u>Career and Relationships</u>: Exploration of how ADHD influences professional paths and personal relationships.

4. *Empowerment and Advocacy*:
- <u>Overcoming Barriers</u>: Many stories might focus on overcoming societal stigma, advocating for proper diagnosis and treatment, and finding empowerment through their journey.
- <u>Raising Awareness</u>: Personal anecdotes can be powerful tools for raising awareness about the specific challenges faced by women with ADHD.

5. *Therapeutic and Diagnostic Insights*:
- <u>Misdiagnosis and Delayed Diagnosis</u>: Common themes often include the journey to a correct diagnosis, especially given the frequent misdiagnosis or late recognition of ADHD in women.
- <u>Treatment Experiences</u>: Varied experiences with different treatment modalities, including medication, therapy, lifestyle changes, and alternative treatments.

6. *Community and Support*:
- <u>Finding Community</u>: Many stories highlight the importance of finding support from others who understand the ADHD experience.
- <u>Role of Support Groups</u>: The benefits of ADHD support groups or online communities in providing advice, comfort, and a sense of belonging.

7. *Personal Growth and Acceptance*:
- <u>Self-Acceptance</u>: Narratives often touch on the journey towards self-acceptance and understanding one's identity with ADHD.
- <u>Growth and Resilience</u>: Reflections on personal growth, resilience, and the development of strengths as a result of navigating life with ADHD.

This chapter would be instrumental in providing readers with real-life insights, fostering a deeper understanding of the female ADHD experience, and offering hope and solidarity to women facing similar challenges.

Interviews: Diverse Experiences of Women with ADHD

Extrapolating meaningful phrases from the interviews of women with ADHD, we can provide a powerful glimpse into their experiences, emotions, challenges, and achievements. Here are some phrases that might be highlighted from such interviews, each capturing the essence of their stories:

- EMILY: ***Embracing the Chaos***

- <u>Experience</u>: "Living with ADHD is like having a browser with too many tabs open – all the time."
- <u>Emotion</u>: "I feel everything intensely, like my emotions are on a rollercoaster without brakes."
- <u>Challenge</u>: "Staying focused at work feels like trying to catch a butterfly in a windstorm."
- <u>Achievement</u>: "I've learned to channel my hyperfocus as a superpower, turning my vibrant ideas into successful projects."

- SARAH: ***The Late Bloomer***

- <u>Experience</u>: "I was the 'daydreamer' – always lost in thought, never quite fitting the mold."
- <u>Emotion</u>: "I often felt misunderstood, like an outsider looking in."
- <u>Challenge</u>: "Organizing my life was a puzzle with missing pieces until my ADHD diagnosis."
- <u>Achievement</u>: "Going back to school and acing my studies was my way of proving that it's never too late to bloom."

- RACHEL: ***The Creative Dynamo***

- <u>Experience</u>: "My mind is a whirlwind of creativity, ideas spinning like a kaleidoscope."
- <u>Emotion</u>: "It's exhilarating yet exhausting, riding the waves of my imagination."
- <u>Challenge</u>: "Finding an outlet for my creativity was challenging; it's easy to start but hard to finish."

- Achievement: "Launching my own art studio was a dream come true – a place where my creativity finds its home."

- **DIANA: *The Resilient Warrior***
- Experience: "Every day is a battlefield, fighting to keep the chaos at bay."
- Emotion: "I've felt the depths of despair but also the heights of triumph."
- Challenge: Balancing motherhood, career, and ADHD is my toughest yet most rewarding battle."
- Achievement: "I've become an advocate for ADHD awareness, turning my struggles into a voice for change."

- **MARGHERITA: *The Social Butterfly***
- Experience: "I thrive in social settings, but it's like dancing on a tightrope with my impulsivity."
- Emotion: "I'm a mosaic of feelings, each social interaction adding a piece to my colorful life."
- Challenge: "Maintaining friendships is tough when you're forgetful and impulsive."
- Achievement: "I've cultivated deep, understanding friendships that see beyond my ADHD."

- **OLIVIA: *The Mindful Maverick***
- Experience: "ADHD adds a layer of complexity to life, like navigating a labyrinth in the dark."
- Emotion: "Mindfulness helps me find peace in the chaos of my mind."
- Challenge: "Staying present and not getting lost in a sea of distractions is a daily practice."
- Achievement: "I've mastered yoga and meditation, teaching others how to find calm amidst their storms."

These phrases encapsulate the diverse experiences and profound resilience of women with ADHD, highlighting their unique challenges and the remarkable ways they overcome them. Each story is a testament to their strength, creativity, and determination to lead fulfilling lives despite the hurdles of ADHD.

Success Stories

This is a list of some well-known individuals who have been diagnosed with or have spoken publicly about their experiences with ADHD:

- **Simone Biles**: She is a gymnast known for her success, having won four Olympic gold medals and 14 world championship medals. ADHD was diagnosed in her childhood, and she takes medication to treat it.

Her adoptive family and a sports psychologist have helped her overcome challenges such as foster care, bullying, and a confidence crisis. She has voiced her opposition to the stigma of ADHD and the hacking of her medical records. Mental health concerns and the 'twisties', which cause disorientation, led her to withdraw from some events at the 2020 Tokyo Olympics.

- **Emma Watson**: Her role as Hermione Granger in the Harry Potter movie has made Emma Watson a well-known actress worldwide. Her struggles with ADHD, a neurological condition that affects millions of people worldwide, have been publicly discussed by her.

Watson's ability to concentrate may have made it possible for her to fully portray her characters and achieve depth in her performances that other actors may struggle to accomplish, and her advocacy for gender equality and women's rights earned her a spot-on Time magazine's 100 Most Influential People in the World list in 2015. Her story exemplifies the unique talents and strengths of individuals with ADHD, despite the challenges of living with it. Her story reinforces the importance of diversity, including neurodiversity, in fostering innovation and strength.

- **Olivia Attwood**: Former Love Island star Olivia Attwood, who has ADHD, shared her experience of being diagnosed as an adult. She described it as a "stroke of luck" to be diagnosed by a psychiatrist specializing in ADHD. Olivia has 'combined' ADHD, which includes symptoms of inattention and hyperactivity-impulsivity. She noted that her unmanaged ADHD in her 20s caused significant stress for those around her.

On her ITVBe show, she revealed that prior to Love Island, she faced severe anxiety, fluctuating depression, and eventually sought help. A specialist later suggested that her undiagnosed ADHD in adulthood might have contributed to her hyperactivity, anxiety, and depression, highlighting the interconnected nature of these conditions.

- **Molly Seidel**: Molly Seidel, an Olympic marathon medalist and mental health advocate, has been open about her struggles with OCD, ADHD, anxiety, depression, and eating disorders.

Diagnosed with OCD while at the University of Notre Dame, she won several NCAA championships before seeking treatment for eating disorders. It was only after her success at the Tokyo Olympics and the 2021 NYC Marathon that she identified ADHD as the root of her mental health challenges. Despite facing criticism online for her ADHD diagnosis, Seidel emphasizes the importance of role models in sports for mental health awareness. She believes the Tokyo Olympics marked a significant moment for mental health in athletics but acknowledges the ongoing stigma and challenges athletes face regarding mental health.

- **Karina Smirnoff**: The professional ballroom dancer known for her appearances on "Dancing with the Stars" has been open about her ADHD diagnosis. At the age of six, she was diagnosed with ADHD. She has been open about her struggles with the condition, and how it has had both positive and negative effects on her life. Smirnoff has stated that her ADHD hinders her ability to concentrate on one thing at a time, and that she is easily distracted.

This has caused her to feel that she is constantly juggling multiple tasks and never actually completing anything. She has stated that her ADHD provides her with a unique energy and creativity that she wouldn't have otherwise. Despite her challenges with ADHD, Smirnoff has found ways to overcome them and has achieved success in both her personal and professional life. Being an advocate for those with ADHD, she emphasizes the importance of finding what works for every person.

Furthermore

- **Michael Phelps**: The most decorated Olympian of all time, Phelps has spoken about his ADHD diagnosis and how swimming helped him channel his energy and focus.
- **Justin Timberlake**: The singer, songwriter, and actor has talked about dealing with ADHD and how it affects his life and career.

- **Adam Levine**: The Maroon 5 frontman and coach on "The Voice" has been vocal about his ADHD, particularly how it continued to affect him into adulthood.
- **Will.i.am**: The musician and founding member of The Black Eyed Peas has discussed his struggles with ADHD, emphasizing how it impacts his creativity.
- **Ty Pennington**: The television host, best known for "Extreme Makeover: Home Edition," has shared his experiences with ADHD, including how it influenced his high energy and creativity.
- **Howie Mandel**: The comedian, actor, and television host has been very open about his ADHD and OCD, using his platform to raise awareness about mental health.

These individuals have used their platforms to raise awareness about ADHD, helping to reduce stigma and demonstrate that success is possible despite the challenges posed by the condition.

Part VI: How to Best Live Daily Life

HOW TO ORGANIZE YOUR HOME

For adults with ADHD, creating an organized home environment requires strategies that cater to their unique needs. Here are several tips that can help:

- ✓ ***Make Your Bed Daily***: Starting with a simple task like making your bed can create a sense of control and lead to developing a mini cleaning routine. It's a manageable step towards a tidier space.

- ✓ ***Break Organizational Tasks into Chunks***: Breaking tasks into smaller steps helps in getting started and reduces feeling overwhelmed. For example, organizing a small number of emails at a time or focusing on one room at a time can be more effective.

- ✓ ***Start-of-Day or End-of-Day Clean***: Cleaning a high-traffic area for 10 to 15 minutes every day helps prevent clutter from building up. This creates a regular routine and avoids the daunting task of extensive cleaning later.

- ✓ ***Find a Permanent Home for Frequently Lost Items***: Designating specific places for items like keys, phones, and wallets helps in reducing time spent searching for them, supporting working memory.

- ✓ ***Use Two Baskets for Clothes***: Having separate baskets for clean and dirty clothes helps keep your bedroom organized and reduces clutter, especially if you don't have time to put clothes away immediately.

- ✓ ***Use Clear Bins for Organization:*** Clear bins are helpful for people with ADHD as they keep items visible and in mind. If clear bins don't suit your style, labeled bins can be an alternative.

✓ *__Use a Planner Regularly:__* Keeping track of deadlines and to-dos in a planner, and checking it frequently, helps in staying organized and remembering important task.

Implementing these strategies can significantly improve organization and reduce the stress associated with clutter in the home for individuals with ADHD.

Managing Clutter and Organize your Daily Life

PILLAR	STRATEGY	DESCRIPTION
ROUTINE	Do One Chore per Day	Schedule 15 minutes daily to tackle a small area, preventing overwhelm
	Finish Something Early in the Day	Complete a small task in the morning for a sense of accomplishment
	Put it in the Calendar	Schedule specific task to increase the likelihood of completion.
	Play it Loose with Deadlines	Allow extra time for tasks to reduce stress.
	Switch Up Cleaning Routine	Change cleaning routine every three months to avoid boredom
Structure	Create a Chore File	Note upcoming chores on index cards and organize them.
	"Think Once" Strategy	Develop a system for recurring tasks like managing mail.
	Get a Grip	Use a physical reminder to stay focused on current tasks.
	Simplify Finishing Steps	Simplify the final steps of a task to maintain interest.
Boundaries	Stop Clutter at the Source	Implement rules to prevent clutter accumulation.
	Designate Junk Drawers	Use specific drawers for miscellaneous items
	Managing the Mail	Reduce and organize mail efficiently.
	Keep Related Items Together	Store related items in the same place to streamline tasks.
Support	Enlist Help	Seek assistance or a **body double** (pag.43) for focus.
	Auto-Pay Bills and Paperless Billing	Automate bill payment to reduce clutter
	Go Professional	Consider hiring a professional organizer in overwhelming situation
The Right Mindset	Allow Yourself to be Wacky	Embrace unique organizing styles.
	Don't worry about "Pretty"	Focus on efficiency over Aesthetics
	Keep Calm and Carry On	Address Major worries first to reduce anxiety
	Leave Room For Improvement	Adopt a mindset of continuous improvement
	Just do it	Start decluttering anywhere without overthinking

SPORT: Recharge your body and mind

Engaging in sports can be particularly beneficial for individuals with ADHD for a variety of reasons. Here's a breakdown of the relationship between sports and ADHD:

Benefits of Sports for ADHD

1. <u>Improved Focus and Concentration</u>: Physical activity increases the levels of dopamine and norepinephrine in the brain, which are neurotransmitters involved in focus and attention. Sports can thus act as a natural stimulant for the ADHD brain.

2. <u>Structure and Routine</u>: Sports often require a consistent schedule for practice and games, providing the structured routine that can be very helpful for someone with ADHD.

3. <u>Physical Energy Outlet</u>: Many individuals with ADHD have excess energy, and sports provide a healthy outlet for expending this energy, which can reduce impulsivity and hyperactivity.

4. <u>Social Skills Development</u>: Team sports offer opportunities to develop social skills, such as cooperation, communication, and understanding social cues.

5. <u>Self-Esteem and Confidence</u>: Mastery of sports skills and achievements in athletic performance can boost self-esteem and confidence.

Types of Sports Suitable for ADHD

1. <u>Team Sports</u>: Soccer, basketball, and hockey can be good for social interaction and developing teamwork skills.

2. Individual Sports: Martial arts, swimming, and track and field can help with self-discipline and individual goal setting.

3. Endurance Sports: Running, cycling, and cross-country skiing can be meditative and help with sustained focus.

4. Sports with a Strong Rhythmic Component: Gymnastics, dance, and climbing can improve coordination and concentration.

Frequency of Participation

Regular participation is key. Most guidelines suggest children should engage in at least 60 minutes of physical activity per day. Adults with ADHD may also find daily exercise beneficial.

Points of Reference
1. <u>Professional Athletes with ADHD</u>: Athletes like Michael Phelps and Simone Biles have ADHD and have achieved great success, serving as role models.
2. <u>Sports Psychology</u>: Working with a sports psychologist can help individuals with ADHD use exercise as a tool for managing symptoms.

Setting Goals
1. <u>SMART Goals</u>: **S**pecific, **M**easurable, **A**chievable, **R**elevant, and **T**ime-bound goals can help individuals with ADHD stay focused and motivated in sports.
2. <u>Incremental Progress</u>: Setting small, incremental goals can lead to a sense of accomplishment and encourage continued participation.
3. <u>Personal Bests</u>: Instead of comparing with others, focusing on personal improvement can be more beneficial and less stressful.

Sports can be a powerful ally in managing ADHD symptoms. The key is to find a sport that the individual enjoys, provides the right level of challenge, and fits into their lifestyle. It's also important to have support, whether from coaches, teammates, or family, to encourage continued participation and to celebrate achievements, no matter how small.

Managing Adhd Symptoms through Sports

Managing ADHD symptoms through sports involves leveraging physical activity to improve cognitive function, emotional well-being, and overall health. Here's how sports can be particularly effective for this purpose:

- ***Enhancing Brain Chemistry***

- <u>Neurotransmitter Regulation</u>: Exercise increases the production of neurotransmitters like dopamine and norepinephrine, which are often at lower levels in individuals with ADHD. These chemicals are crucial for attention and processing speed, and their increase can lead to improved attention and mood.

- <u>Endorphin Release</u>: Physical activity triggers the release of endorphins, the body's natural mood lifters. This can be especially beneficial for those with ADHD who may experience mood swings or depression.

- **Improving Executive Function**
- <u>Boosting Working Memory</u>: Sports that require strategy and quick decision-making can enhance working memory. This is the system we use for temporarily storing and managing information.

- <u>Enhancing Cognitive Flexibility</u>: Switching between tasks and strategies during a game can improve cognitive flexibility, helping individuals with ADHD to better transition between tasks in daily life.

- **Reducing Symptoms**
- <u>Decreasing Hyperactivity</u>: Engaging in regular physical activity provides an outlet for excess energy, which can reduce hyperactivity and impulsivity.
- <u>Improving Sleep</u>: Regular exercise can help regulate sleep patterns, which is often a challenge for those with ADHD. Better sleep can lead to improvements in attention and behavior.

- **Structuring the Day**
- <u>Routine Building</u>: Sports can help in establishing a routine, which can provide a sense of stability and predictability. This is particularly helpful for individuals with ADHD who may struggle with time management and organization.

- **Social and Emotional Benefits**
- <u>Social Skills Development</u>: Team sports can teach the importance of teamwork, communication, and social interaction, which can be challenging for some with ADHD.
- <u>Stress Relief</u>: Physical activity is a proven stress reliever. For individuals with ADHD, who may experience higher levels of stress, sports can be an effective coping mechanism.

- ***Self-Image and Self-Efficacy***

- <u>Building Confidence</u>: Achieving goals in sports can build self-esteem and a sense of accomplishment, which can counteract feelings of frustration or failure that may come with ADHD.
- <u>Developing Discipline</u>: Training for sports can foster discipline and self-control, which can translate into other areas of life.

Practical Tips for Incorporating Sports into ADHD Management

- *<u>Choose Enjoyable Activities</u>*: It's important to select sports that are enjoyable, as this increases the likelihood of sustained participation.
- *<u>Consistent Schedule</u>*: Try to maintain a consistent schedule for physical activities to build a routine.
- *<u>Set Realistic Goals</u>*: Start with achievable goals to avoid discouragement and gradually increase the challenge.
- *<u>Use Technology</u>*: Fitness trackers and apps can provide reminders and motivation to stay active.
- *<u>Involve Peers or Family</u>*: Working out with others can provide additional motivation and accountability.

Incorporating sports into the management of ADHD can be a holistic approach to improving symptoms. It's not just about the physical benefits; it's also about creating a balanced lifestyle that supports mental and emotional well-being. As with any new regimen, it's advisable to start slowly and consult with healthcare providers, especially when making significant changes to physical activity levels.

Music: Get in ecstasy with the right sound

Music can be a powerful tool for individuals with ADHD, offering various benefits that can help manage symptoms and improve quality of life. Here's a general overview of how music can be beneficial for a woman with ADHD:

Benefits of Music for Women with ADHD:

1. Improved Focus: Certain types of music, especially instrumental or classical pieces, can enhance concentration and help minimize distractions.
2. Reduced Anxiety: Music with a slow tempo can be soothing and may reduce anxiety and stress levels, which are often heightened in individuals with ADHD.
3. Enhanced Mood: Upbeat and cheerful music can boost dopamine levels, improving mood and motivation, which can be particularly helpful for those with ADHD.
4. Better Sleep: Soft, calming music can be used as part of a bedtime routine to help signal the brain that it's time to wind down, leading to improved sleep quality.
5. Structured Routine: Music can serve as a time-keeping tool, helping to structure tasks and transitions throughout the day.

Frequency and Kind of Music:

- ***Frequency***: Listening to music can be incorporated into daily routines, but the frequency can vary depending on the individual's preferences and the task at hand. Some may benefit from music throughout the day, while others might find it helpful only during specific activities, like work or relaxation.
- ***Kind of Music***: The type of music that may be beneficial can vary widely. Some general suggestions include:
- **For Focus**: Instrumental or classical music, such as pieces by Bach or Mozart, or even ambient sounds.
- **For Relaxation**: Slow tempo music, nature sounds, or white noise.
- **For Mood Enhancement**: Upbeat and energetic music, which can vary depending on personal taste.
- **For Sleep**: Soft, lyrical, or non-lyrical music with a slow beat.

It's important to note that music preferences are highly individual, and what works for one person may not work for another. Women with ADHD should experiment with different types of music to see what best supports their needs and preferences. Additionally, the volume and environment in which music is played can also affect its efficacy; for some, a quiet background track might be beneficial, while others may prefer a more immersive experience with headphones.

The Suitable Place for the Music

The best place to listen to music for someone with ADHD can vary greatly depending on individual preferences and the specific activity they are engaged in. Here are some general suggestions:

1. *Private, Controlled Environments*: For tasks that require focus, such as studying or working, a private room where the individual can control the sound level and minimize interruptions may be ideal.

2. *Nature Settings*: For relaxation and stress relief, listening to music outdoors, such as in a park or garden, can be beneficial. The natural setting can enhance the calming effects of music.

3. *During Exercise*: Listening to music while walking, running, or engaging in other forms of exercise can be motivating and help maintain a rhythm in physical activities.

4. *In the Car*: For some, the car can be a great place to listen to music. It can help make the commute more enjoyable and can serve as a transition tool between home and work or school.

5. *Through Headphones*: Using headphones, especially noise-cancelling ones, can help create a personal space free from external distractions, which can be particularly helpful in public spaces or busy households.

6. *In a Dedicated Music Room*: If available, a room dedicated to relaxation and music listening, with comfortable seating and pleasant lighting, can enhance the listening experience.

7. *Before Bed*: In the bedroom before sleep, listening to calming music can be part of a healthy bedtime routine to signal the brain that it's time to wind down.

It's important for individuals with ADHD to consider what they are trying to achieve with music listening (e.g., focus, relaxation, motivation) and to adjust their environment accordingly. It's also beneficial to be mindful of the volume to ensure that it's not contributing to overstimulation. Experimentation is key, as personal preference will play a significant role in determining the best place to listen to music.

Hobbies: Unleash your creativity and inner strength

Women with ADHD often find hobbies and creative pursuits particularly rewarding, as these activities can provide a positive outlet for their energy, offer sensory stimulation, and allow for the expression of their unique perspectives. Here are some common hobbies, arts, and creative activities that women with ADHD might enjoy:

1. *Artistic Endeavors*:
   - <u>Painting and Drawing</u>: These activities can be soothing and offer a way to visually express emotions and thoughts.
   - <u>Photography</u>: Capturing moments can be a satisfying way to focus attention and create lasting memories.
   - <u>Sculpture</u>: Working with hands to mold materials can be a tactile and engaging activity.

2. *Crafting*:
   - <u>Knitting and Crocheting</u>: These repetitive activities can be meditative and provide a sense of accomplishment.
   - <u>Jewelry Making</u>: Designing and creating jewelry can be a detailed, absorbing task that results in wearable art.
   - <u>Scrapbooking</u>: Organizing photos and memorabilia into albums can be a creative way to document life events.

3. *Performing Arts*:
   - <u>Dance</u>: Movement can be a powerful way for women with ADHD to connect with their bodies and emotions.
   - <u>Theater</u>: Acting can provide an outlet for creativity and an opportunity to explore different personas.
   - <u>Music</u>: Playing an instrument or singing offers a structured yet expressive hobby.

4. *Writing*:
   - <u>Creative Writing</u>: Crafting stories or poetry can be a form of emotional release and self-expression.
   - <u>Blogging</u>: Sharing experiences or interests through a blog can provide a sense of community and purpose.

5. *Gardening*:
   - <u>Flower Gardening</u>: Growing and tending to plants can be therapeutic and offers immediate, tangible results.
   - <u>Vegetable Gardening</u>: This can be rewarding and also provide a sense of self-sufficiency.

6. *Cooking and Baking*:
   - <u>Experimenting with Recipes</u>: Trying new recipes can be a creative and rewarding challenge.
   - <u>Baking</u>: The precision required for baking can be satisfying for those who enjoy following detailed steps to create something delicious.

7. *DIY Projects*:
   - <u>Home Decor</u>: Creating or repurposing items can give a sense of personalization and control over one's environment.
   - <u>Furniture Restoration</u>: Bringing new life to old pieces can be a fulfilling project that requires focus and creativity.

8. *Physical Activities*:
   - <u>Yoga</u>: The combination of physical movement and mindfulness can be beneficial for self-regulation.
   - <u>Martial Arts</u>: These disciplines offer a structured way to develop focus and physical control.

9. *Digital Arts*:
   - <u>Graphic Design</u>: Using software to create digital art can be a modern way to express creativity.
   - <u>Video Editing</u>: Creating videos can be an engaging way to tell stories and share experiences.

10. *Collecting*:
   - <u>Collectibles</u>: Gathering items of interest can be a passionate hobby that involves research and knowledge.

Women with ADHD may gravitate towards hobbies that offer immediate feedback, allow for hyperfocus, or provide a sensory experience. It's important for hobbies to be flexible and forgiving, as rigid structures can sometimes be challenging for those with ADHD. The key is to find activities that are enjoyable, play to their strengths, and offer a sense of accomplishment and satisfaction.

Healthy Eating: Refuel your brain.

The relationship between food and women with ADHD is an important aspect to consider, as diet can impact energy levels, mood, and ADHD symptoms. Here's a general overview of how food can relate to women with ADHD:

1. **Healthy Foods**:

   - Protein-Rich Foods: Protein can promote the production of neurotransmitters like dopamine, which is often in short supply in ADHD brains. Including protein in each meal can help with focus and energy levels. Examples include lean meats, fish, eggs, dairy, nuts, and legumes.

   - Complex Carbohydrates: Foods like whole grains, fruits, and vegetables can provide a steady source of energy and help manage blood sugar levels, which can, in turn, help regulate mood and energy.

   - Omega-3 Fatty Acids: These are thought to support brain health and may help alleviate ADHD symptoms. Foods high in omega-3s include fish like salmon and mackerel, flaxseeds, chia seeds, and walnuts.

2. **Foods to Avoid**

   - Simple Sugars and High Glycemic Index Foods: These can cause spikes and crashes in blood sugar levels, which may exacerbate ADHD symptoms.

   - Artificial Additives: Some studies suggest that certain food colorings and preservatives may increase hyperactivity in some children with ADHD, although the evidence is not conclusive.

   - Allergens and Sensitivities: Some individuals with ADHD might be sensitive to certain foods, like gluten or dairy, which could potentially affect behavior and focus.

3. **Quantity and Type of Meals**:

   - Regular, Balanced Meals: Eating at regular intervals can help maintain blood sugar levels, which can reduce mood swings and improve focus.

-Smaller, More Frequent Meals: Some find that smaller meals spaced throughout the day can help manage energy levels and prevent overeating.

4. **When to Eat**:
   - Consistent Meal Times: Having a routine can be helpful for managing ADHD symptoms. Eating at consistent times aids in regulating the body's internal clock.
   - Mindful Eating: Paying attention to hunger cues and eating slowly can prevent overeating and help with digestion.

5. **Hydration**:
   - Adequate Water Intake: Staying hydrated is crucial for cognitive function and overall health. Sometimes, what feels like hunger is actually dehydration.

6. **Planning and Preparation**:
   - Meal Planning: Women with ADHD may benefit from planning meals in advance to avoid decision fatigue and ensure a balanced diet.
   - Meal Prepping: Preparing meals ahead of time can help avoid impulsive food choices and make it easier to eat healthily.

7. **Mindful Eating Practices**:
   - Attention to Eating: Being present during meals, rather than eating while distracted, can help with portion control and enjoyment of food.
   - Listening to the Body Tuning into signals of hunger and fullness can prevent overeating and help identify food sensitivities.

8. **Supplements**:
   - Consultation with a Professional: Before starting any supplements, it's important for women with ADHD to consult with a healthcare provider, as some supplements can interact with ADHD medications or have side effects.

It's important to note that while diet can play a role in managing ADHD symptoms, it is not a substitute for professional medical treatment. Women with ADHD should work with healthcare providers to determine the best comprehensive approach for managing their symptoms, which may include medication, therapy, lifestyle changes, and dietary adjustments.

Open Space: Enjoy in your Home

Living in a home environment that supports ADHD can make a significant difference in managing symptoms and enhancing daily functioning. Here are some pointers tailored for women with ADHD to help create a home that facilitates focus, organization, and a sense of calm:

1. **Arrangement of Furniture**:
   - <u>Defined Spaces</u>: Create distinct areas for different activities, such as a reading nook, a workspace, and a relaxation zone. This can help with transitioning between tasks.
   - <u>Minimize Clutter</u>: Keep furniture to a necessary minimum to reduce visual clutter, which can be distracting.
   - <u>Functional Organization</u>: Use furniture with built-in storage to keep items out of sight but within reach.

2. **Kitchen Equipment**:
   - <u>Clear Countertops</u>: Keep counters as clear as possible to reduce visual noise and make it easier to start tasks like cooking.
   - <u>Organized Storage</u>: Use drawer dividers, clear containers, and labels to make ingredients and tools easy to find.
   - <u>Time-Saving Appliances</u>: Consider appliances that save time and simplify cooking, like slow cookers, instant pots, or pre-programmed coffee makers.

3. **Work Equipment**:
   - <u>Ergonomic Furniture</u>: Invest in a comfortable, supportive chair and a desk at the right height to encourage longer periods of focus.
   - <u>Good Lighting</u>: Ensure ample lighting to reduce eye strain. Natural light is ideal, but if that's not possible, use full-spectrum light bulbs.
   - <u>Visual Task Lists</u>: Keep a whiteboard or bulletin board to visually manage tasks and deadlines.

4. **Household Items**:
   - <u>Dual-Purpose Items</u>: Choose items that serve more than one purpose to reduce the need for multiple products and save space.
   - <u>Easy Maintenance</u>: Select furnishings and textiles that are easy to clean and maintain.

- _Color Coding_: Use color to categorize items, such as towels or bedding, to quickly identify what goes where.

5. **Organization Systems**:
- _Open Shelving_: Use open shelves with baskets or bins to organize items by category, making them easy to access and put away.
- _Label Everything_: Clearly label shelves, bins, and drawers to remind you where things belong.
- _Routine Checkpoints_: Establish spots for frequently lost items, like keys or phones, near the entrance or in the bedroom.

6. **Decor**:
- _Calming Colors_: Use soothing colors that promote relaxation and concentration, especially in areas for work or sleep.
- _Personal Touches:_ Incorporate items that make you happy and motivated, like artwork, plants, or personal mementos.
- _Adaptable Spaces_: Have areas that can be easily rearranged to suit different activities or moods.

7. **Technology**:
- _Smart Home Devices_: Consider smart plugs, lights, and thermostats to automate routine tasks and reduce the cognitive load.
- _Noise Control_: Use white noise machines or noise-canceling headphones to minimize auditory distractions.

8. **Routine and Structure**:
- _Visual Schedules_: Display calendars and clocks prominently to keep track of time and routines.
- _Consistent Layout_: Try to keep the layout consistent to avoid confusion and create a sense of stability.

9. **Relaxation Zones**:
- _Dedicated Quiet Area_: Create a space for relaxation and unwinding, free from work or household chores.
- _Comfort Items_: Have blankets, cushions, or a yoga mat available for comfort and stress relief.

10. **Safety and Accessibility**:
   - <u>Safe Storage</u>: Keep dangerous or toxic items in high or locked cabinets.
   - <u>Accessibility</u>: Ensure that frequently used items are easily accessible to avoid the frustration of searching.

Remember, the goal is to create a living space that reduces stress and distraction while promoting efficiency and comfort. It's also important to be flexible and adjust the environment as needed, since the effectiveness of these strategies can change over time.